A LANGUAGE GUIDE FOR SELF-STUDY

Learning Chinese

Speak, Read and Write Chinese with Manga!

HAOHSIANG LIAO

TUTTLE Publishing

Tokyo │Rutland, Vermont│ Singapore

Contents

LESSON 1
A Basic Introduction

The world's languages are all thought to belong to five major language families: Indo-European, Sino-Tibetan, Niger-Congo, Afro-Asiatic and Austronesian. Chinese, along with many other languages spoken in Asia, like Burmese and Tibetan, is a member of the Sino-Tibetan family.

The modern form of Chinese spoken in China today was developed in the early 20th century to serve as a "national language" to help people from all over China to communicate with each other more easily. Nowadays everyone in China learns the language when they go to school, and almost everyone can speak it—although some older people have difficulty speaking it clearly (but they understand).

Chinese is different from the classical Chinese used in ancient China and also very different from the various regional Chinese languages still spoken throughout the country today—although these languages do share common roots and similarities. (For example, the same written characters are used in all the Chinese languages even though the vocabulary and grammar may differ.) Chinese is as different from Cantonese, Shanghainese or Szechuanese as English is from German, French or Italian. Many people in China speak their local regional language at home and with close friends but they speak Chinese at school, at work and in more formal situations. Often they mix the two together into a sort of colorful mash-up which can be very entertaining.

Chinese today has the most native speakers of any language in the world. It is the official language of Mainland China, Taiwan and Hong Kong, and one of the four official languages of Singapore. In Mainland China it is referred to as **Pǔtōnghuà** (the "common" or "everyday" language) or **Zhōngwén** (the "Chinese language"). In Taiwan, it is called **Guóyǔ** (the "national language") while in Singapore it is **Huáyǔ** (another way of saying the "Chinese language").

Chinese syllables and words
Chinese words consist of one or more syllables, just like English words. Each Chinese syllable has a main vowel with a tone marking placed above it (see below) plus one or more consonants at the beginning or end of the syllable (or both). For instance, **shū** means "book" in Chinese: "**sh**" is the initial consonant and "**ū**" is the vowel with the tone mark above it. More examples:

hē	drink
ān	peace
ài	love

áo	suffer
jiào	called
fēng	wind
sòng	give

The majority of Chinese words have one or two syllables. Several examples of single-syllable words are:

chá	tea
máng	busy
wǒ	I

Some examples of words with two syllables are:

xuésheng	student
lánqiú	basketball
Běijīng	Beijing

Two single-syllable words, each with their own meaning, are joined together to form a compound Chinese word. In Chinese almost all two-syllable words are formed this way. Learning the single syllable words and then learning all the various compounds is a very good way of expanding your Chinese vocabulary. Here are some examples:

diàn "electricity" + **fèi** "fee"	= **diànfèi** "electricity bill"
huǒ "fire" + **chē** "vehicle"	= **huǒchē** "train"
jiā "family" + **rén** "person(s)"	= **jiārén** "family members"
shì "try" + **chuān** "wear"	= **shìchuān** "try on"
shū "book" + **diàn** "store"	= **shūdiàn** "bookstore"

The Hànyǔ Pīnyīn Romanization System

Another characteristic of Chinese is that the Chinese characters for the words do not tell you exactly how they are pronounced (although some clues are given). In fact, many characters are pronounced exactly the same way! For example:

shī: "master" 师, "wet" 湿, "lion" 狮, "poem" 诗
fēng: "wind" 风, "crazy" 疯, "seal" 封, "harvest" 丰
máng: "busy" 忙, "blind" 盲, "bandit" 氓

In addition, some characters have more than one sound. For instance:

都：(1) **dū** as in **shǒudū** "capital city", (2) **dōu** "all"
觉：(1) **jué** as in **juéde** "feel", (2) **jiào** as in **shuìjiào** "sleep"
便：(1) **pián** as in **piányi** "cheap", (2) **biàn** as in **fāngbiàn** "convenient"

It is nearly impossible to write Chinese using a purely phonetic system of writing—because many words would look and sound the same and the intended meaning would be unclear without referring to the characters. Traditionally, in fact, no alphabetic system existed at all. However, in modern times a standard romanization system was developed to teach school children and foreigners to pronounce the characters. This standard system was developed by the Mainland Chinese government in late 1950s and is called *Hanyu Pinyin* (often referred to simply as *Pinyin*). Other systems of romanization exist, but *Pinyin* has become the standard method of writing Chinese phonetically and has been widely adopted for educational purposes, along with computer and mobile phone input editors.

Install a *Pinyin* keyboard on your keyboard or mobile phone and type in the *Pinyin* word (e.g., **ma**). A list of possible Chinese characters corresponding to that sound will appear (e.g., **mà** "scold", or **ma** "question marker" or **mā** "mother"). For words with two syllables or more, type "**mm**" to produce words like **māma** "mother" or **mèimei** "younger sister".

The way the letters of the alphabet are pronounced in *Hanyu Pinyin* is quite similar to English, with the following exceptions:

Examples:

a always has the British pronunciation as in "<u>a</u>unt" not "<u>a</u>nt" — **āyí** (aunt)

q is pronounced like the "**ch**" in "<u>ch</u>eek" — **qí** (ride)

x is pronounced like the "**sh**" in "<u>sh</u>een" — **xiā** (prawn)

z is pronounced like the "**dz**" in "a<u>dz</u>e" — **zì** (word)

c is pronounced like "**ts**" in "ca<u>ts</u>" — **cóng** (from)

g is always hard as in "<u>g</u>uard" or "ba<u>g</u>" (never like in "ra<u>g</u>e" or "<u>g</u>eneral") — **gěi** (give)

zh is pronounced like the "**dg**" in "e<u>dg</u>e" — **zhè** (this)

sh is pronounced like the "**sh**" in "<u>sh</u>irt" — **shǒu** (hand)

r is pronounced like the "**r**" in "<u>r</u>ain" — **rè** (hot in temperature), similar to the pronunciation in English except less round.

ü is pronounced like the "**ui**" in "acq<u>ui</u>t" — **yǔ** (rain)

uo is pronounced like the "**a**" in "w<u>a</u>r" — **shuō** (speak)

un is pronounced like the "**w**" in "<u>w</u>on" in combination with "**en**" — **chūn** (spring)

Please listen to the accompanying audio recordings to familiarize yourself with the pronunciations of all the various sounds in Chinese.

Also note that in sentences Chinese characters are written with no spacing between the words. However, when they are written in *Pinyin*, we follow the Western way of spacing words. So for example the expression "I am American" in Chinese characters is 我是美国人 with no space between 我 (**wǒ** or "I"), 是 (**shì** "am"), 美国 (**Měiguó** "America"), and 人 (**rén** "person"). In *Pinyin*, it is written as **Wǒ shì Měiguó rén** with spaces to separate the words.

Tones

Tones are used in Chinese to distinguish words which have the same sound but different meanings. There are four tones in Chinese: the first tone, the second tone, the third tone, and the fourth tone. Please refer to the audio recordings and read the notes below to understand how these tones are pronounced. For example:

mā "mother"   high, even tone
má "numb"   starts mid-low, and rises to a higher intonation.
mǎ "horse"   starts mid-low, drops to low and then rises
mà "to scold"   sharp tone, dropping from a mid-high tone to a mid-low tone

The First Tone

The first tone is high, flat and long. Do keep the high pitch from the beginning to the end. If you drop toward the end, it will sound like the fourth tone. Examples are **mā** (mother) and **xī** (west).

The Second Tone

The second tone is rising slowly from low to high. Do not start your pitch too low and do "climb-up." Examples are **má** (numb) and **xí** (mat).

The Third Tone

The third tone dips first and then rises. Start from a mid-tone, drop to low and then rise. You can consider doubling the vowel if it helps (e.g., **maa** or **xii**). Examples are **mǎ** (horse) and **xǐ** (to wash).

The Fourth Tone

The fourth tone falls sharply from high to low. This tone is similar to the English imperatives such as "Go!" or "Run!" Examples are **mà** (to scold) and **xì** (thin).

Many people think the tones are difficult to learn, but actually they are not that difficult. All you have to do is listen to them over and over a few times until you can hear the difference. And when you learn a new word, try to learn the tone at the same time.

A Few Things to Remember about Tones

1. A full third tone first drops and then rises again slowly, but in everyday speech when people speak quickly, the third tone is rarely pronounced fully. Instead, it just sounds like a low tone or sounds like it's dipping down a little.

2. When two consecutive words in a sentence both have the third tone, the first one changes to a rising tone (second tone). For example: **hěn hǎo** becomes **hén hǎo** (very good).

3. A tone mark is placed above the main vowel of a syllable when it is written in *Pinyin* even though the tone applies to the entire syllable and not just the vowel.

4. When there are two vowels in a syllable, the tone mark is normally placed above the first one, as in **pǎo** (run) and **shòu** (skinny). The exceptions to this are when the first vowel is an **i** or **u** at the end of a word. In this case, the tone mark goes above the second vowel, as in **tiě** (iron) and **xué** (to learn).

5. When a syllable ends with a vowel and is joined in a compound to another syllable that begins with a vowel, an apostrophe is often inserted in between the two vowels when it is written in *Pinyin* to avoid confusion. For example: **Xī'ān** (the name of a Chinese city) and **nǚ'ér** (daughter). But these can also be written without the apostrophe (as **Xīān** and **nǚér**).

The Neutral Tone

In addition to the four active tones, there is also a neutral tone (or really lack of tone in Chinese), which is mainly used for very short words that are skipped over and pronounced very quickly. This includes words which mainly indicate punctuation—for example **le** (indicating a completed action) and **ma** (indicating a question). As the name suggests, the neutral tone is unstressed and does not have any tone mark. Words with the neutral tone rarely appear on their own; they are usually the unstressed second or last syllable of a word where the first syllable carries the tone, such as **xuésheng** (student) and **háizi** (children). Here are some other examples of syllables with neutral tones (i.e., no tones):

dōngxi	thing	**kèqi**	polite	**shénme**	what
jiǎozi	dumpling	**piányi**	cheap		

Audio Recordings

Audio recordings are available online for each lesson's Dialogue, Vocabulary, Pattern Practices and Exercises. Please refer to the inside cover for details on how to access these.

* Wrong pronunciation. It should be sì.

LESSON 2
The Basics

Terms of Address
The basic terms of address in Chinese are:

Singular

Pinyin	English
wǒ	I
nǐ	you
nín	you (polite)
tā	he/she

Plural

Pinyin	English
wǒmen	we
zánmen	we (inclusive, used in Northern China)
nǐmen	you
tāmen	they

Titles as Terms of Address

Pinyin	English
Xiānsheng	Mr.
Xiáojie	Ms.
Nǔshì	Mrs.
jīnglǐ	manager
jiàoshòu	professor
lǎoshī	teacher
shīfu	taxi driver (**sījī xiānsheng** in Taiwan)
fúwùyuán	waiter/waitress (**xiānsheng/xiáojie** in Taiwan)

Common Question Expressions

Pinyin	English
Shénme	What
Shénme shíhou	When
Shéi	Who
Nǎ(r)	Where
Jǐdiǎn	What time
Zěnmele	What's wrong?/What happened?
Duōshǎo qián	How much (money)
Jǐsuì	How old (under ten)
Duō dà	How old (above ten)

Duōcháng shíjiān	How long (time)
Zěnme ...	How (to ...)
... Zěnmeyàng	How about ...

Numbers

Pinyin	English
líng	zero
yī	one
èr	two
sān	three
sì	four
wǔ	five
liù	six
qī	seven
bā	eight
jiǔ	nine
shí	ten
bǎi	hundred
qiān	thousand
wàn	ten thousand
bǎiwàn	million
yì	hundred million

Common Stative Verbs

Pinyin	English
piányi	cheap
jìn	close (distance)
lěng	cold
fāngbiàn	convenient
guì	expensive
yuǎn	far
hǎo	good
gāoxìng	happy
rè	hot (temperature)
yǒu yìsi	interesting
piàoliang	pretty
hǎochī	tasty
lèi	tired

Common Place Names

Pinyin	English
Běijīng	Beijing
Chéngdū	Chengdu
Guǎngzhōu	Guangzhou
Hángzhōu	Hangzhou
Xiānggǎng	Hong Kong
Nánjīng	Nanjing
Shànghǎi	Shanghai
Shēnzhèn	Shenzhen
Táiběi	Taipei
Xī'ān	Xi'an

Basic Sentence Structures

In general, there are two sentence structures in Chinese. The first one is "Subject + Verb + Object" as in English. For example:

Subject	Verb	Object	
Wǒ	shì	Peter.	I am Peter.
Wǒ	shì	Měiguó rén.	I am (an) American.
Wǒ	xǐhuan	Zhōngguó wénhuà.	I like Chinese culture.

The second structure is the "Topic + Comment," prominent in conversations when the topic is mentioned and is obvious to the interlocutors. For instance:

Topic	Comment	
Zhōngguó cài	wǒ dōu xǐhuan.	I like all Chinese dishes.
Zhèixiē zì	wǒ rènshi.	I know these (written) characters.

Behavioral Culture

In this book, besides developing the ability to participate in simple, practical conversations on everyday topics, you will also develop an understanding of Chinese interpersonal behavioral culture and related thought patterns. Aside from teaching you the language, we will also include notes on the proper behavior in Chinese culture. Remember, cultural norms are as important as linguistic forms.

LESSON 3
Greetings

Eric Goodman, an American college student studying Chinese history at Tsinghua University in Beijing, bumps into his new Chinese friend, Li Yang, on campus.

Yang:	Hi, Gao Zhi'an (Eric's Chinese name). **Gāo Zhì'ān, nǐ hǎo.** 高志安,你好。
Eric:	Hi, Li Yang, how are you? Where are you going? **Èh, Lǐ Yáng, nǐ hǎo. Nǐ qù nǎr?** 欸,李洋,你好。 你去哪儿?
Yang:	I am going to buy some things. What about you? **Wǒ qù mǎi yìdiǎn(r) dōngxi. Nǐ ne?** 我去买一点儿东西。 你呢?
Eric:	I am going to the dining hall. **Wǒ qù shítáng.** 我去食堂。
Yang:	Okay, see you. **En, zàijiàn.** 嗯,再见。
Eric:	See you. **Zàijiàn.** 再见。

New Vocabulary

Pinyin	Chinese Character	English
Nǐ	你	You (singular)
Nǐ hǎo	你好	Hi; how are you, literally, "you good"?
Èh	欸	Hey; hi, also to acknowledge the speaker
Nǎ(r)	哪儿	Where
Wǒ	我	I
Qù	去	Go; go to
Mǎi	买	Buy
Yìdiǎn(r)	一点儿	A little, some
Dōngxi	东西	Thing
Ne	呢	How about, what about
Shítáng	食堂	Dining hall, cafeteria
En	嗯	Indicates agreement
Zàijiàn	再见	Goodbye, see you

CULTURAL NOTE Chinese Names

The order of Chinese names is Surname + Given name. When you hear a Chinese name (e.g., **Gāo Zhì'ān**), it is safe to assume that **Gāo** is the surname and **Zhì'ān** is the given name. Most Chinese surnames have only one syllable, such as **Lǐ, Lín, Wáng, Zhāng,** and **Gāo.** Chinese given names may have one or two syllables (e.g., **Zhì'ān** for Eric Goodman, and **Yáng** for Li Yang). Many Chinese who are living in the West may invert their names so the given name precedes the surname.

CULTURAL NOTE Common Greetings

The many different greetings vary according to the situation, the time of the day, or the people you are conversing with. **Nǐ hǎo** is a more formal greeting used when meeting someone for the first time or if you have recently become acquainted with that person. Address persons who are older or of a higher status using their title, such as **jīnglǐ** or "manager", **lǎoshī** or "teacher". Informal greetings such as "What's up" should only be used with very close friends or family members.

Supplementary Vocabulary Place names

Pinyin	English
shūdiàn	bookstore
kāfēidiàn	coffee shop
gōngsī	company
túshūguǎn	library
bàngōngshì	office
wèishēngjiān	restroom, toilet
shāngdiàn	store
Běijīng Dàxué	Peking University
Qīnghuá Dàxué	Tsinghua University

Note: **Běijīng Dàxué** and **Qīnghuá Dàxué** are the top two universities in Mainland China. Due to historical reasons, you will find one Tsinghua University in Beijing and the other one in Hsinchu, Taiwan.

GRAMMAR NOTE The Verb **Qù** = "To Go"

Just as in English, the verb **qù** in Chinese can be used in different ways:

1. **qù + a place word** means "go to [a place]." For instance, if you want to say "go to a dining hall" you can say **qù shítáng**. More examples:

qù shūdiàn	go (to a) bookstore
qù wèishēngjiān	go (to the) restroom
qù Běijīng Dàxué	go (to) Peking University

2. **qù + a verb phrase** indicates purpose (going to [do something]). For instance **qù mǎi yìdiǎnr dōngxi** means "I'm going to buy a few things." More examples:

qù mǎi kāfēi	go buy coffee
qù chīfàn	go eat
qù shàngbān	go (to) work

Figure out the timing by inferring from the sentence, context or from time and dates mentioned (see Lesson 6) in the sentence, as Chinese lacks word indicating tenses.

Helpful Tip: Changing Tones: Tone 3 + Tone 3 = Tone 2 + Tone 3
Whenever two words with Tone 3 appear in succession the tone of the first word changes to Tone 2 + Tone 3. If you listen to the audio recordings carefully, the tones for **nǐ hǎo** are actually **ní hǎo**. More examples:

hěn hǎo (very good)	becomes	**hén hǎo**
mǎi bǐ (buy pens)	becomes	**mái bǐ**

Helpful Tip: The Interjection Èh = "Hey" or "Hi"
Èh is often used when you want to talk about something or get someone's attention.

GRAMMAR NOTE The Question Word **Nǎr** = "Where?"

Form a question in Chinese by replacing the subject of your inquiry (e.g., **shítáng** or "dining hall" in the sentence **Tā qù shítáng** or "He is going to the dining hall") with the corresponding question word such as "Where?" Thus the sentence becomes **Tā qù nǎr?** The question word is usually placed at the end of the sentence and the order of the words in the sentence does not change. More examples:

Gāo Zhì'ān qù nǎr?	Where is Gao Zhi'an going?
Lǐ Yáng qù nǎr?	Where is Li Yang going?

CULTURAL NOTE The Optional "**r**" Sound

People in northern China generally pronounce this "**r**" sound more than southerners.

GRAMMAR NOTE The Particle **Ne** = "How/What About"

The particle **ne**—usually following a pronoun or noun phrase—is used at the end of a sentence to recap or shorten a repeated question. More examples:

Gāo Zhì'ān qù shítáng, Lǐ Yáng ne?
Gao Zhi'an is going to the dining hall. What about Li Yang?

Nǐ qù Qīnghuá Dàxué, tā ne?
You are going to Tsinghua University. What about him/her?

GRAMMAR NOTE   **The Interjection En**

The interjection **En** indicates that the person has heard your statement and agrees with what you're saying, or is acknowledging what you've said.

Pattern Practice 1

Practice saying the following phrases.
qù + a place word

qù shítáng	go to the dining hall
qù shūdiàn	go to a bookstore
qù wèishēngjiān	go to the restroom
qù Qīnghuá Dàxué	go to Tsinghua University

Pattern Practice 2

Practice saying the following phrases.
qù + a verb phrase

qù mǎi dōngxi	go buy things
qù chīfàn	go to eat
qù shàngbān	go to work

Pattern Practice 3

Practice saying the following phrases.
Subject + **qù nǎr**

Nǐ qù nǎr?	Where are you going?
Tā qù nǎr?	Where is he/she going?
Gāo Zhì'ān qù nǎr?	Where is Gao Zhi'an going?

Pattern Practice 4

Pronoun/Noun + **ne**

Tā ne?	What about him/her?
Wǒ ne?	What about me?
Gāo Zhì'ān ne?	What about Gao Zhi'an?
Lǐ Yáng ne?	What about Li Yang?

EXERCISE SET 1

Fill in each blank with one of the following expressions.

ne	nǐ hǎo	nǎr	zàijiàn

1. A: Èi, nǐ hǎo.
   B: _____.

2. A: Nǐ qù _____?
   B: Wǒ qù shítáng.

3. A: Wǒ qù mǎi yìdiǎnr dōngxi, nǐ _____?
   B: Wǒ qù túshūguǎn.

4. A: Wǒ qù mǎi yìdiǎnr dōngxi, zàijiàn.
   B: _____.

EXERCISE SET 2

Translate the following dialogues into Chinese.

1. A: Hey, how are you?
   B: Hi, where are you going?
   A: I am going to the bookstore. How about you?
   B: I am going to the dining hall.

2. A: Hey, where are you going?
   B: I am going to buy some things. What about you?
   A: I am going to eat.
   B: Okay, see you.
   A: See you.

EXERCISE SET 3

Role Playing

You are an exchange student to Shanghai from the United States. You bump into your new Chinese friend, Li An, on campus on your way to the grocery store. Greet him warmly and ask him where he is going.

LESSON 4
Introducing Yourself (I)

DIALOGUE Self-Introductions

Wang Min, an undergraduate student at Tsinghua University in Beijing, is sitting in the library across the table from Eric Goodman. Out of curiosity, she decides to strike up a conversation with him.

Min:	Hi, what is your name?
	Nǐ hǎo, nǐ jiào shénme míngzi?
	你好, 你叫什么名字?
Eric:	My name is Gao Zhi'an. What is yours?
	Wǒ jiào Gāo Zhì'ān, nǐ ne?
	我叫高志安, 你呢?
Min:	My name is Wang Min. What country are you from?
	Wǒ jiào Wáng Mǐn. Nǐ shì něiguó rén?
	我叫王敏。 你是哪国人?
Eric:	I am an American. Are you a student, too?
	Wǒ shì Měiguó rén. Nǐ yě shì xuésheng ma?
	我是美国人。 你也是学生吗?
Min:	Yes, I am studying English. How about you?
	Duì, wǒ xué Yīngyǔ, nǐ ne?
	对, 我学英语, 你呢?
Eric:	I study Chinese history.
	Wǒ xué Zhōngguó lìshǐ.
	我学中国历史。

New Vocabulary

Pinyin	Chinese Character	English
Jiào	叫	To be called or named
Shénme	什么	What
Míngzi	名字	Name
Wáng Mǐn	王敏	Wang Min, a full name where Wang is the surname and Min the first name
Shì	是	To be
Něi-	哪	Which?
Něiguó	国人	Which country?
Rén	人	Person, people
Měiguó	美国	America
Měiguó rén	美国人	An American
Yě	也	Also, too
Xuésheng	学生	Student

New Vocabulary (cont'd)

Pinyin	Chinese Character	English
Ma	吗	(Indicates a question)
Duì	对	Correct, right
Xué	学	To study, learn
Yīngyǔ	英语	The English language
Zhōngguó	中国	China
Lìshǐ	历史	History

GRAMMAR NOTE   The Verb **Jiào** = "To be Called, To be Named"

The verb **jiào** is commonly used when asking someone's name or telling someone your name. You would say **Wǒ jiào Gāo Zhì'ān** in Chinese, which literally means "I am named/called Gao Zhi'an." More examples:

Tā jiào Lǐ Yáng.	His name is Li Yang.
Wǒ jiào Wáng Mǐn, nǐ ne?	My name is Wang Min. What about you?

GRAMMAR NOTE   The Verb **Shì** = "To be"

Shì is a verb in Chinese meaning "to be." So "I am an American" is **Wǒ shì Měiguó rén** in Chinese. Likewise, "He is Chinese" is **Tā shì Zhōngguó rén**. More examples:

Gāo Zhì'ān shì xuésheng.	Gao Zhi'an is a student.
Gāo Zhì'ān shì Měiguó rén.	Gao Zhi'an is American.
Wáng Mǐn shì Zhōngguó rén.	Wang Min is Chinese.

The verb **shì** is omitted in Chinese in many situations where we would use "to be" in English, particularly when followed by an adjective. It would be ungrammatical to use **shì** in this case as it would mean "I am equal to tired". We'll address this point in a later lesson.

GRAMMAR NOTE   The Question Word **Shénme** = "What?"

Shénme is an important question word meaning "what?" It can be used both in front of and after a thing being referred to, as in the following examples:

Nǐ jiào shénme míngzi?	What is your name?
Nǐ mǎi shénme?	What are you buying?
Nǐ xué shénme?	What do you study?

GRAMMAR NOTE   The Question Word **Něi-** = "Which?"

The question word **něi-** meaning "which?" needs to be followed by a measure word (we'll introduce the measure words in detail in Lesson 5) in Chinese to form a question. In the sentence **Nǐ shì něiguó rén?** which means "Which country are you from?" the word **guó** is a measure word meaning "country" or "nationality" and **něiguó rén** means "person of which country?"

The other variation in pronunciation of **něi** is **nǎ**, so **Nǐ shì něiguó rén** is equivalent to **Nǐ shì nǎguó rén**. Generally, **něi** is more commonly used by people in northern China while others use **nǎ**. Do not confuse **něi** with **nǎr**—**něi** needs to be followed by a measure word whereas **nǎr** does not.

GRAMMAR NOTE   The Question Word **Ma**

Adding the Chinese word **ma** at the end of a simple statement is like adding a question mark in English, and is a way to form a simple yes-no question in Chinese. **Nǐ shì xuésheng** "You are a student" is a simple statement whereas **Nǐ shì xuésheng ma?** "Are you a student?" is a question. Similarly, **Nǐ shì Zhōngguó rén** "You are Chinese." is a statement whereas **Nǐ shì Zhōngguó rén ma?** "Are you Chinese?" is a question. More examples:

Nǐ qù túshūguǎn ma?	Are you going to the library?
Lǐ Yáng qù chīfàn ma?	Is Li Yang going to eat?

Helpful Tip:
When adding **ma** at the end, a rising intonation on the last syllable is normally used to indicate that you are asking a question.

GRAMMAR NOTE   Using the Word **Yě** = "Also, too"

The adverb **yě** which means "also" must precede the main verb of the sentence and not be placed after it, i.e., "I, too, am a student". So "I am a student, too" or "I am also a student" in Chinese becomes **Wǒ yě shì xuésheng**, rather than **Wǒ shì yě xuésheng** or **Wǒ shì xuésheng yě**. More examples:

Lǐ Yáng shì Zhōngguó rén, Wáng Mǐn yě shì Zhōngguó rén.
Li Yang is Chinese, and Wang Min is also Chinese.

Gāo Zhì'ān qù shítáng, wǒ yě qù shítáng.
Gao Zhi'an is going to the dining hall, so am I.

GRAMMAR NOTE   Chinese Has No Articles Like "A" or "The"

Notice that the English word "a" in the sentence "I am a student" is dropped in Chinese. So you say **Tā shì lǎoshī** to mean "He/She is *a* teacher."

Supplementary Vocabulary Country names

Pinyin	English
Àodàlìyà	Australia
Jiā'nadà	Canada
Yīngguó	England
Fǎguó	France
Déguó	Germany

Rìběn	Japan
Hánguó	Korea
Tàiguó	Thailand
Yuènán	Vietnam

CULTURAL NOTE **Talking About Your Nationality**

To indicate a nationality you simply take the country name and add the word **rén** (person) to it. So "a Chinese person" is **Zhōngguó rén** and "an American" is **Měiguó rén**. Please refer to the vocabulary above for more country names. To all of these countries' names you simply add the word **rén** in order to get the nationality:

Àodàlìyà rén: Australian = an Australian person
Jiā'nádà rén: Canadian = a Canadian person
Yīngguó rén: British = an English person
Rìběn rén: Japanese = a Japanese person

CULTURAL NOTE **The Word Zhōngguó = "China" or "Chinese"**

The word **Zhōngguó** refers to the country of China, but the word can also mean "Chinese" or "China-related", such as **Zhōngguó lìshǐ** "Chinese history" or **Zhōngguó cài** "Chinese food". When referring to the written Chinese language, another word, **Zhōngwén**, is used.

College Majors and Subjects

Pinyin	English
Shēngwùxué	Biology
Huàxué	Chemistry
Diànnǎo kēxué (Jìsuànjī kēxué)	Computer Science
Jīngjìxué	Economics
Jīnróng	Finance
Shùxué	Mathematics
Wùlǐ	Physics
Zhèngzhìxué	Political Science
Xīnlǐxué	Psychology
Zhōngwén	Chinese

GRAMMAR NOTE   The Verb **Xué** = "To Study, Learn"

The verb **xué** meaning "to study" is used in the names of many fields of study as in the above list. It needs to be followed by the subject or topic that one is studying, such as:

Wǒ xué Yīngyǔ.	I study (major in) English.
Wǒ xué lìshǐ.	I study (major in) History.
Wǒ xué diànnǎo kēxué.	I study (major in) Computer Science.

Pattern Practice 1

Practice saying the following phrases.
Subject + **jiào** + name

Tā jiào Lǐ Yáng.	His name is Li Yang.
Tā jiào Gāo Zhì'ān.	His name is Gao Zhi'an.
Wǒ jiào Wáng Mǐn.	My name is Wang Min.

Pattern Practice 2

Practice saying the following phrases.
Subject + **shì** + noun

Wǒ shì Měiguó rén.	I am American.
Tā shì Zhōngguó rén.	He/She is Chinese.
Tā shì Hánguó rén.	He/She is Korean.
Wáng Mǐn shì xuésheng.	Wang Min is a student.

Pattern Practice 3

Practice saying the following phrases.
Statement + **ma**

Tā jiào Lǐ Yáng ma?	Is his name Li Yang?
Nǐ shì Měiguó rén ma?	Are you American?
Lǐ Yáng qù chīfàn ma?	Is Li Yang going to eat?
Wáng Mǐn shì xuésheng ma?	Is Wang Min a student?
Wáng Mǐn xué Yīngyǔ ma?	Does Wang Min study English?

Pattern Practice 4

Practice saying the following phrases.
Subject + **yě** + verb phrase

Wǒ yě shì Měiguó rén.	I am also American.
Wǒ yě qù mǎi dōngxi.	I am also going to buy things.
Nǐ yě xué Zhōngwén.	You are also studying (the) Chinese language.
Tā yě jiào Wáng Mǐn.	Her name is also Wang Min.
Gāo Zhì'ān yě shì xuésheng.	Gao Zhi'an is also a student.

EXERCISE SET 1

Fill in each blank with one of the following expressions.

shì	jiào	ma	yě

1. **Nǐ hǎo, nǐ _____ shénme míngzi?**

2. **Nǐ hǎo, nǐ _____ něiguó rén?**

3. A: **Wǒ shì Měiguó rén.**
   B: **Wǒ _____ shì Měiguó rén.**

4. A: **Nǐ xué Zhōngguó lìshǐ _____ ?**
   B: **Duì, wǒ xué Zhōngguó lìshǐ.**

EXERCISE SET 2

Answer each of the following questions in Chinese.

1. **Nǐ jiào shénme míngzi?**
2. **Nǐ shì něiguó rén?**
3. **Nǐ xué shénme?**

EXERCISE SET 3

Translate the following sentences into Chinese.

1. A: Hi, what's your name?
    B: My name is Wang Min, and yours?
    A: My name is Li Yang.

2. A: Hi, which country are you from?
    B: I am German. What about you?
    A: I am Japanese. What do you study?
    B: I study the Chinese language.
    A: Me too.

EXERCISE SET 4

Role Playing

You are an exchange student at Tsinghua University in Beijing. Today is the first day of your Chinese history class. You decide to strike up a conversation with the classmate sitting next to you. Greet your classmate first and then inquire about his/ her name, nationality and major.

Tsinghua University, Beijing

LESSON 5
Introducing Yourself (II)

▦ DIALOGUE ▦ Asking Questions

Eric Goodman has questions about one of his classes. He decides to stop by the professor's office after class.

Eric:	Hi, Professor Zhang, I am an exchange student from the History Department. My name is Gao Zhi'an. **Zhāng Lǎoshī, nín hǎo, wǒ shì lìshǐxìde jiāohuàn xuésheng, wǒ jiào Gāo Zhì'ān.** 张老师, 您好, 我是历史系的交换学生, 我叫高志安。
Professor Zhang:	Hi, how can I help you? **Nǐ hǎo, yǒu shìr ma?** 你好, 有事儿吗?
Eric:	I'd like to ask you a question. **Wǒ xiǎng qǐng wèn nín yíge wèntí.** 我想请问您一个问题。
Professor Zhang:	Sure, please have a seat. **Hǎo, qǐng zuò.** 好, 请坐。
Eric:	Thank you. **Xièxie.** 谢谢。
Professor Zhang:	You are welcome. **Bié kèqi.** 别客气。

New Vocabulary

Pinyin	Chinese Character	English
Lǎoshī	老师	Teacher
Nín	您	You (Polite form, singular)
Xì	系	Department
-De	的	Descriptive -**de** (see grammar note "The Descriptive Word -**de** = 's)
Jiāohuàn	交换	Exchange (*n*)
Yǒu	有	Have
Shì(r)	事儿	Thing, matter
Xiǎng	想	Would like to, want to
Qǐng	请	Please
Wèn	问	Ask

New Vocabulary (cont'd)

Pinyin	Chinese Character	English
Yī	一	One or a
Ge	个	(Measure word)
Wèntí	问题	Question (n)
Hǎo	好	Okay, sure
Zuò	坐	Sit
Xièxie	谢谢	Thank you
Bié kèqi	别客气	You are welcome

Supplementary Vocabulary   Common Chinese Last Names

Pinyin	English
Chén	Chen
Gāo	Gao
Huáng	Huang
Lǐ	Li
Lín	Lin
Liú	Liu
Wáng	Wang
Wú	Wu
Yáng	Yang
Zhāng	Zhang

CULTURAL NOTE   Terms of Address

Using the correct form of address in Chinese is important. You have learned a few terms of address in Chinese in Lesson 2, such as **xiānsheng** (Mr.), **xiáojie** (Ms), **lǎoshī** (teacher) and **jiàoshòu** (professor). To address people in Chinese, you put their surname first and then the term of address. Thus, you'd say "**Zhāng Lǎoshī**" in Chinese when addressing "teacher Zhang" and not **Lǎoshī Zhang**. Likewise, "Professor Lǐ" in Chinese is **Lǐ Jiàoshòu**, not **Jiàoshòu Lǐ**.

In Chinese culture, it is common to address people of higher social status simply by their titles, such as **xiānsheng**, **xiáojie**, and **lǎoshī**. Thus, when you encounter your Chinese teacher Professor Zhang on campus, you can nod and greet him/her, "**lǎoshī**" or "**lǎoshī hǎo**." Avoid saying just **nǐ hǎo** to your teacher as the term is used mostly for people of similar social status who meet for the first time.

Jiàoshòu is the word for college professors whereas **lǎoshī** is for teachers in general. College students in Chinese societies also address their professors as **lǎoshī**.

GRAMMAR NOTE   ### Requesting Something Appropriately **Qǐng +** **Verb = "Please (Verb)"**

Chinese people frequently use "qǐng + verb" pattern to make their request more polite, especially to people of higher social status. **Qǐng wèn** (Please ask) sounds more polite than simply saying **wèn**. More examples:

Qǐng zuò.   Please be seated.
Qǐng jiào tā Lǐ Jiàoshòu.   Please call him/her Professor Li.

GRAMMAR NOTE   ### The Honorific Word **Nín = "You"**

Nín is used to address people of higher status, such as **lǎoshī** (teacher) or **jīnglǐ** (manager). Notice that **nín**, like other pronouns in Chinese, can function both as a subject, e.g., **nín hǎo** (polite form of "Hello") and as an object e.g., **wèn nín** (ask you).

Similarly, **wǒ** can mean "I" or "me." Eric says **nín hǎo** to Professor Zhang while Professor Zhang says **nǐ hǎo** to Eric. Examples of when **nín** can be used as a subject can include:

Zhāng Jiàoshòu, nín hǎo.   Hello, Professor Zhang.
Wáng Xiáojie, nín hǎo mā?   Ms Wang, how are you?

Examples of when **nín** can be used as an object include:

Wǒ xiǎng qǐng wèn nín yíge wèntí.   I would like to ask you a question.
Tā jiào nín Lǐ Jiàoshòu ma?   Does he call you Professor Li?

GRAMMAR NOTE   ### The Descriptive Word **De = 's**

The descriptive -**de** is used to show the affiliation of the preceding words and what follows. These phrases should be said without any pause in your speech. For example:

Wǒ shì Qīnghuá Dàxuéde xuésheng.
I am a student of Tsinghua University.

Wǒ shì Yīngyǔxìde xuésheng.
I am a student in the English Department.

GRAMMAR NOTE   The Verb **Yǒu** = "Have"

This verb means "have". Examples include:

Nǐ yǒu Zhōngwén míngzi ma?	Do you have a Chinese name?
Nǐ yǒu shìr ma?	Can I help you?
Zhāng Lǎoshī yǒu Měiguó xuésheng ma?	Does Professor Zhang have American students?

GRAMMAR NOTE   The Auxiliary Verb **Xiǎng** = "Would like to"

It is often used when a speaker of lower social status makes a request to someone of higher social level. **Xiǎng** is appropriate to use in this situation as the student has a question for his teacher.

Wǒ xiǎng qǐng wèn nín yíge wèntí.	I would like to ask you a question.
Wǒ xiǎng xué Zhōngguó lìshǐ.	I want to study Chinese history.
Wǒ xiǎng qù wèn Zhāng Lǎoshī yíge wèntí.	I would like to go and ask Professor Zhang a question.

Helpful Tip: Number + Measure Word + Noun

As mentioned before, a noun in Chinese can be either singular or plural, so **Wǒ yǒu wèntí** can mean "I have a question" or "I have questions." To specify *one* question, you will need to use the "Number + Measure Word + Noun" pattern. In the dialogue, we introduced the most general measure word **ge** in Chinese. So if you want to say "I have one Chinese teacher," it is **Wǒ yǒu yíge Zhōngwén lǎoshī.**

Helpful Tip: The Word **Yī** = "One"

With the first tone, **yī** refers to the number and digit "one". When **yī** is followed by a word with a syllable using Tone 1, 2, or 3, it will change its tone to Tone 4, such as in the example **Wǒ qù mǎi yìdiǎnr dōngxi** ("I'm going to buy *some* things") in Lesson 3.

However, when **yī** is followed by a syllable with a neutral tone or Tone 4, it needs to be changed to **yí**, such as in **Wǒ yǒu yíge Zhōngwén lǎoshī** ("I have one Chinese teacher"). More examples:

yíge Zhōngwén míngzi	a Chinese name
yíge shítáng	a dining hall
yíge túshūguǎn	a library
yíge dōngxi	a thing

Helpful Tip: The Word **Hǎo** Indicates Agreement

You have learned **hǎo** meaning "good" in Lesson 3, such as **nǐ hǎo** "Hi, how are you." **Hǎo** in this lesson indicates agreement and is often used alone as a response to a request. For example:

A: **Qǐng jiào tā Lǐ Jiàoshòu.**   Please call him/her Professor Li.
B: **Hǎo.**   Okay.

Helpful Tip: The Idiomatic Response "**Bié Kèqi**"

This expression is a common response to **xièxie**. Another variation of **bié kèqi** is **bú kèqi** which literally means "Don't (need to be so) polite."

Pattern Practice 1

Practice saying the following phrases.
Subject + **shì** + noun 1 + **de** + noun 2

Wǒ shì lìshǐxìde xuésheng.   I am a student from the History Department.

Tā shì Yīngyǔxìde xuésheng.   He/She is a teacher at Peking University.

Tā shì Běijīng Dàxuéde lǎoshī.   He/She is a student from the English Department.

Lǐ Yáng shì Qīnghuá Dàxuéde xuésheng.   Li Yang is a student at Tsinghua University.

Pattern Practice 2

Practice saying the following phrases.
Subject + **yǒu** + noun

Wǒ yǒu Zhōngwén míngzi.   I have a Chinese name.
Wáng Mǐn yǒu Yīngwén míngzi.   Wang Min has an English name.
Nǐ yǒu shìr ma?   Can I help you?
Zhāng Lǎoshī yǒu Rìběn xuésheng ma?   Does Professor Zhang have Japanese students?

Pattern Practice 3

Practice saying the following phrases.
Number + **ge** + noun

yíge wèntí	a question
yíge lǎoshī	a teacher
yíge míngzi	a name
yíge péngyǒu	a friend

EXERCISE SET 1

Fill in each of the following blanks with the proper word or phrase.

qǐng	Bié kèqi	Nín hǎo	de	ge

1. A: **Zhāng Lǎoshī, _____.**
   B: **Nǐ hǎo.**

2. **Wǒ shì Yīngyǔxì _____ xuésheng, wǒ jiào Wáng Mǐn.**

3. **Lǎoshī, wǒ xiǎng _____ wèn nín yí _____ wèntí.**

4. A: **Qǐng zuò.**
   B: **Xièxie.**
   A: **_____.**

EXERCISE SET 2

Translate the following dialogues into Chinese.

1. A: Hi Teacher, my name is Lǐ Lì. I am an exchange student from the Physics Department.
   B: Hi, how are you?

2. A: Teacher, I would like to ask you a question.
   B: Sure. Please have a seat.

3. A: Teacher, thank you very much.
   B: You are welcome. Bye.
   A: Bye.

EXERCISE SET 3
Role Playing

You have just finished your first economics class at Tsinghua University in Beijing. You have a question for the professor. Approach the professor, introduce yourself, and then politely ask your question.

LESSON 6
Small Talk

Li Yang bumps into his American friend Eric Goodman on campus. They haven't seen each other for a few days.

Yang:	Gao Zhi'an, how have you been recently?
	Gāo Zhì'ān, nǐ zuìjìn zěnmeyàng?
	高志安，你最近怎么样？
Eric:	Pretty good. How about you?
	Hái xíng, nǐ ne?
	还行，你呢？
Yang:	Pretty busy. Do you want to play basketball together tomorrow?
	Tǐng mángde. Èh, míngtiān yìqǐ dǎ lánqiú zěnmeyàng?
	挺忙的。唉，明天一起打篮球怎么样？
Eric:	What time tomorrow? I have something to do tomorrow morning.
	Míngtiān jǐdiǎn? Míngtiān shàngwǔ wǒ yǒu yìdiǎnr shìr.
	明天几点？明天上午我有一点儿事儿。
Yang:	What about tomorrow afternoon at 4 o'clock then?
	Nà, xiàwǔ sìdiǎn zěnmeyàng?
	那，下午四点怎么样？
Eric:	Sounds good. See you tomorrow.
	Hǎo, míngtiān jiàn.
	好，明天见。
Yang:	See you tomorrow.
	Míngtiān jiàn.
	明天见。

New Vocabulary

Pinyin	Chinese Character	English
Zuìjìn	最近	Recently; lately
Zěnmeyàng	怎么样	How, how about
Hái	还	Still
Xíng	行	Okay, all right (*v*)
Tǐng...de	挺...的	Pretty, very
Máng	忙	Busy
Míngtiān	明天	Tomorrow
Yìqǐ	一起	Together
Dǎ	打	Play (*v*)
Lánqiú	篮球	Basketball
Jǐ-	几	How many

New Vocabulary (cont'd)

Pinyin	Chinese Character	English
Diǎn	点	O'clock
Jǐdiǎn	几点	What time
Shàngwǔ	上午	Morning, a.m.
Nà	那	Then, in that case
Xiàwǔ	下午	Afternoon, p.m.
Sì	四	Four
Míngtiān jiàn	明天见	"See you tomorrow"

Supplementary Vocabulary Time Words

Pinyin	English
Jīntiān	Today
Hòutiān	The day after tomorrow
Zuótiān	Yesterday
Qiántiān	The day before yesterday
Zhōngwǔ	Noon
Wǎnshàng	Evening
Xiànzài	Now

GRAMMAR NOTE The Expression **Zěnmeyàng** = "How are You Doing?"

Zěnmeyàng is a useful expression and it has two usages. One serves as a common way of greetings to ask acquaintances or friends how they are doing, such as **Nǐ zěnmeyàng** ("How are you doing?"). **Zěnmeyàng** is too casual and is inappropriate for greeting your elders or persons of higher social status. More examples:

Gāo Zhì'ān, nǐ zuìjìn zěnmeyàng?	Gao Zhi'an, how have you been recently?
Lǐ Yáng, Wáng Mǐn zuìjìn zěnmeyàng?	Li Yang, how is Wang Min recently?

The other usage of **zěnmeyàng** is to elicit opinions. For example:

Míngtiān dǎ lánqiú zěnmeyàng?	How about playing basketball tomorrow?
Wǒmen qù kāfēidiàn zěnmeyàng?	Let's go to a coffee shop, how about that?
Xiàwǔ sìdiǎn zěnmeyàng?	How about 4 o'clock in the afternoon?

GRAMMAR NOTE Using the Expression **Hái Xíng** = "Pretty Good"

Hái xíng is composed of **Hái** (still) and **xíng** (good, O.K.). It can be translated into "still hanging on there," "pretty good," "still O.K.," or "so-so." It is used mainly in northern China and not so often used in Taiwan. People in Taiwan would say **Hái kéyǐ** or literally "still can".

GRAMMAR NOTE **Using the Pattern Tǐng...De = "Pretty" or "Very"**

Tǐng...de, used mainly in northern China in an informal setting, means "pretty" or "very". Thus, you can compliment your Chinese friend on his/her English by saying **Nǐde Yīngyǔ tǐng hǎode** ("Your English is pretty good"). More examples:

Gāo Zhì'ānde Zhōngwén tǐng hǎode.   Gao Zhi'an's Chinese is pretty good.
Wáng Mǐn tǐng kèqide.   Wang Min is pretty polite.

GRAMMAR NOTE **Using the Adverb Yìqǐ = "Together"**

The adverb **yìqǐ** needs to be placed after the subject and in front of the verb in Chinese. So if you want to invite your friend to go shopping, you can say **Wǒmen míngtiān yìqǐ qù mǎi dōngxi, zěnmeyàng?** ("Let's go shopping together tomorrow. How about that?") More examples:

Wǒmen yìqǐ qù mǎi kāfēi.   Let's go and buy coffee together.
Tāmen yìqǐ qù chīfàn.   They are going to eat together.

GRAMMAR NOTE **Using the Verb Dǎ = "Hit with Hands"**

The literal meaning of **dǎ** is "hit with hands." **Qiú** means "ball" and **dǎ lánqiú** means "play basketball." Other sports that go with the verb **dǎ** in Chinese include:

dǎ bàngqiú	play baseball
dǎ páiqiú	play volleyball
dǎ pīngpāngqiú	play ping pong
dǎ wǎngqiú	play tennis
dǎ yǔmáoqiú	play badminton

GRAMMAR NOTE **Using Time Words in Chinese**

Note the location of the time word **míngtiān** in the sentence **Míngtiān yìqǐ dǎ lánqiú zěnmeyàng?** In Chinese, a time word needs to be placed either in the beginning of a sentence or between the subject and the verb. So if you want to say "We will play basketball together tomorrow," you should say **Míngtiān wǒmen yìqǐ dǎ lánqiú** or **Wǒmen míngtiān yìqǐ dǎ lánqiú.** Remember, it is incorrect to put the time phrase at the end of the sentence as in **Wǒmen yìqǐ dǎ lánqiú míngtiān.** More examples:

Wǒmen jīntiān wǎnshàng yìqǐ qù mǎi dōngxi.   Let's go buy things together tonight.

Hòutiān wǒ xiǎng qù wèn Zhāng Lǎoshī yíge wèntí.   I want to go and ask Professor Zhang a question the day after tomorrow.

Míngtiān jiàn "See you tomorrow" is another good example to show that the time word **míngtiān** comes before the main verb **jiàn**.

GRAMMAR NOTE Using the Expression **Jǐdiǎn** = "What Time"

The literal meaning of **jǐ** is "how many" and **diǎn** is "o'clock." To ask "What time is it now?" you can say **Xiànzài jǐdiǎn? Diǎn** is a measure word that must follow the numeral even when the context is clear, that is, **sìdiǎn** "four o'clock" or **shídiǎn** "ten o'clock" rather than just **sì** "four" or **shí** "ten".

GRAMMAR NOTE Using the Word **Nà** in Turn-Taking

Nà, in this case, is equivalent to "then" or "in that case". It is a good word to use between speakers in turn-taking. It gives the speaker extra time to come up with what follows, such as an alternative suggestion, in this case.

CULTURAL NOTE Big Units Before Small Units

Note the structure of the phrase **míngtiān jǐdiǎn**. The big unit **míngtiān** comes before the small unit **jǐdiǎn**. It would be ungrammatical to reverse the order and say **jǐdiǎn míngtiān**. To follow this rule, "tomorrow morning" is **míngtiān shàngwǔ** and "tomorrow afternoon" is **míngtiān xiàwǔ**. The big unit before small unit principle also applies to the order of Chinese names (surname + given name) and Chinese addresses (city + street + section + house/apartment number + floor).

Pattern Practice 1

Practice saying the following phrases.
Topic + **zěnmeyàng**

Tā zěnmeyàng?	How is he/she doing?
Nǐ zuìjìn zěnmeyàng?	How have you been doing?
Míngtiān dǎ lánqiú zěnmeyàng?	How about playing basketball tomorrow?
Wǒmen qù kāfēidiàn zěnmeyàng?	Let's go to a coffee shop. How about that?
Wǒmen qù Zhōngguó zěnmeyàng?	Let's go to China. How about that?

Pattern Practice 2

Practice saying the following phrases.
Subject + **tǐng...de**

Wǒ tǐng mángde.	I am pretty busy.
Tāmen yě tǐng mángde.	They are also pretty busy.
Lǐ Yáng tǐng kèqide.	Li Yang is pretty polite.
Zhōngwén tǐng nánde.	The Chinese language is pretty difficult.

Pattern Practice 3

Practice saying the following phrases.
Subject + **yìqǐ** + verb phrase

Wǒmen yìqǐ qù mǎi dōngxi.	Let's go buy things together.
Wǒmen yìqǐ qù chīfàn.	Let's go eat together.
Tāmen yìqǐ xué Zhōngwén.	They study Chinese together.
Wǒmen yìqǐ qù wèn Zhāng Lǎoshī.	Let's go ask Professor Zhang together.

Pattern Practice 4

Practice saying the following phrases.
Jǐ/Number + **diǎn**

Jǐdiǎn?	What time?
Sāndiǎn	Three o'clock
Qīdiǎn	Seven o'clock
Jiǔdiǎn	Nine o'clock
Shí'èrdiǎn	Twelve o'clock

Pattern Practice 5

Practice saying the following phrases.
Subject + time word + verb phrase

Wǒmen míngtiān dǎ lánqiú.	We will be playing basketball tomorrow.
Wǒmen míngtiān dǎ pīngpāngqiú.	We will be playing ping pong tomorrow.
Wǒmen jīntiān wèn Zhāng Lǎoshī.	We are asking Professor Zhang today.
Wǒmen jīntiān qù Běijīng Dàxué.	We are going to Peking University today.
Gāo Zhì'ān sìdiǎn xué Zhōngwén.	Gao Zhi'an studies Chinese at four o'clock.
Zhāng Lǎoshī hòutiān qù Měiguó.	Professor Zhang is going to the US the day after tomorrow.

EXERCISE SET 1

Fill in each blank with one of the following expressions.

yìqǐ	jǐ	zěnmeyàng	tǐng

1. A: Nǐ _____?
   B: Hái xíng.

2. A: Nǐ máng ma?
   B: _____ mángde.

3. A: Wǒmen _____ qù mǎi dōngxi, zěnmeyàng?

4. A: Xiànzài _____ diǎn?
   B: Sāndiǎn.

EXERCISE SET 2

Answer each of the following questions in Chinese.

1. Nǐ zuìjin zěnmeyàng?
2. Xiànzài jǐdiǎn?
3. Nǐ míngtiān shàngwǔ yǒu shìr ma?

EXERCISE SET 3

Translate the following dialogues into Chinese.

1. A: Hey, how have you been?
   B: Pretty good. How about you?
   A: I am pretty busy.

2. A: Hey, let's play volleyball together tomorrow. How about that?
   B: Sounds good. What time tomorrow?
   A: Three o'clock in the afternoon.
   B: Okay, see you tomorrow.
   A: See you.

3 A: What time do you go to eat?
   B: Twelve o'clock.
   A: Great. Let's go together.
   B: Okay.

EXERCISE SET 4

Role Play

You are an exchange student studying at Tsinghua University in Beijing. You are thinking about doing some grocery shopping tomorrow. Ask your Chinese roommate if he/she wants to go with you.

Chinese supermarkets carry a wide range of products.

LESSON 7
Getting Around

Finding Places

When playing basketball, Eric Goodman asks Li Yang about the location of the swimming complex on campus.

Eric:	Li Yang, do you know where the swimming complex is on campus?
	Lǐ Yáng, xuéxiàode yóuyǒngguǎn zài nǎr?
	李洋,学校的游泳馆在哪儿?
Yang:	It's next to the sports center. Do you know where the sports center is?
	Zài yùndòng zhōngxīn de pángbiān. Nǐ zhīdào yùndòng zhōngxīn zài nǎr ma?
	在运动中心的旁边。你知道运动中心在哪儿吗?
Eric:	I do. Is the swimming complex open today?
	Zhīdào. Yóuyǒngguǎn jīntiān kāi ma?
	知道。游泳馆今天开吗?
Yang:	Today is Sunday, so it's not open.
	Jīntiān shì xīngqītiān, suóyi bù kāi.
	今天是星期天,所以不开。
Eric:	What time will it be open tomorrow then?
	Nà míngtiān jǐdiǎn kāi?
	那明天几点开?
Yang:	I don't know either. You can take a look on the Internet.
	Wǒ yě bù zhīdào. Nǐ kéyi shàngwǎng kàn yíxià.
	我也不知道。你可以上网看一下。
Eric:	Okay.
	Hǎo.
	好。

New Vocabulary

Pinyin	Chinese Character	English
Xuéxiào	学校	School
-De	的	(Indicates possession)
Yóuyǒngguǎn	游泳馆	Swimming complex (**yóuyǒng** "swimming/swim", **guǎn** "building, hall")
Zài	在	Be located at
Yùndòng	运动	Exercise, sports; to exercise
Zhōngxīn	中心	Center
Pángbiān	旁边	Next to, on the side of
Zhīdào	知道	Know

New Vocabulary (cont'd)

Pinyin	Chinese Character	English
Kāi	开	Open (*v*)
Xīngqītiān	星期天	Sunday
Suóyi	所以	So
Bù	不	Not; negation marker
Kéyi	可以	Can, may
Shàngwǎng	上网	Go online
Kàn	看	See, look
-Yíxià	一下	A little, a while (*verb softener*)

Supplementary Vocabulary   More Place Words

Pinyin	English
Duìmiàn	Across (**miàn** "on the surface of")
Lǐmiàn	Inside
Wàimiàn	Outside
Shàngmiàn	On the top
Xiàmiàn	On the bottom
Zuǒbiān	On the left (**biān** "on the side of")
Yòubiān	On the right
Zhōngjiān	In the middle

GRAMMAR NOTE   The Marker -**De** = 's Indicating Possession

In Lesson 5, you have learned the descriptive **de** to show the affiliation of what precedes and what follows, such as **Wǒ shì lìshǐxìde xuésheng** ("I am a student from the History Department"). In this lesson, -**de** functions as a possession marker. Examples:

Wǒde lǎoshi	My teacher
Nǐde míngzi	Your name
Zhāng Lǎoshīde xuésheng	Professor Zhang's students
Xuéxiàode yóuyǒngguǎn	The school's swimming complex

GRAMMAR NOTE   Place Words as Subject

A place word often serves as the subject in a sentence in Chinese. Examples:

Yùndòng zhōngxīn zài nǎr?	Where is the sports center?
Yóuyǒngguǎn jīntiān kāi ma?	Is the swimming complex open today?
Yóuyǒngguǎn míngtiān bù kāi.	The swimming complex is not open tomorrow.
Yóuyǒngguǎn zài yùndòng zhōngxīnde pángbiān.	The swimming complex is next to the sports center.

GRAMMAR NOTE   The Word **Zài Nǎr** = "Where"

In Chinese, if you want to inquire about the location of a place, you use the "place + zài nǎr" pattern. Examples:

Yóuyǒngguǎn zài nǎr?	Where is the swimming complex?
Xuéxiàode shítáng zài nǎr?	Where is the dining hall on campus?
Qīnghuá Dàxué zài nǎr?	Where is Tsinghua University?
Lǐ Yáng xiànzài zài nǎr?	Where is Li Yang right now?

To respond, you simply replace **nǎr** with a place word. Examples:

Yóuyǒngguǎn zài (nǐde) pángbiān.	The swimming complex is next (to you).
Qīnghuá Dàxué zài Běijīng.	Tsinghua University is in Beijing.
Xuéxiàode shítáng zài (nǐde) duìmiàn.	The dining hall on campus is across (from you).

You can further identify the location by adding a place word between **zài** and **pángbiān**. Examples:

Yóuyǒngguǎn zài yùndòng zhōngxīnde pángbiān.	The swimming complex is next to the sports center.
Túshūguǎn zài yùndòng zhōngxīnde duìmiàn.	The library is across from the sports center.
Lǐ Yáng xiànzài zài xuéxiàode yùndòng zhōngxīn.	Li Yang is now at the sports center on campus.

GRAMMAR NOTE   The Word **Zhīdào** = "Know (Facts or Things)"

Zhīdào refers to knowing facts or things; it is rarely used to refer to recognizing or knowing people. Examples:

Wǒ zhīdào tāde míngzi.	I know his/her name.
Qǐng wèn, nǐ zhīdào xiànzài jǐdiǎn ma?	Excuse me, do you know what time it is now?

Note that a short response to the question **nǐ zhīdào … ma?** is **zhīdào**, simply repeating the main verb in the question. You can also say **Wǒ zhīdào** ("I know"). Similarly, if Eric Goodman is asked **Nǐ shì xuésheng ma?** ("Are you a student?"), he can answer **Shì** or **Wǒ shì** to mean "Yes, I am."

GRAMMAR NOTE Using The Negation Word **Bù** = "Not"

In Chinese, except for **yǒu** (have), you can negate a verb or a stative verb by adding **bù** in the front. Examples:

bù hǎo	not good
bù zhīdào	not know
bù kāi	not open
Wǒde Zhōngwén bù hǎo.	My Chinese is not good.
Yóuyǒngguǎn jīntiān bù kāi.	The swimming complex is not open today.
Wǒ bù zhīdào yùndòng zhōngxīn zài nǎr.	I don't know where the sports center is.

Helpful Tip: Changing Tones of Bù

When the verb following **bù** is Tone 1, 2, or 3, **bù** is Tone 4, such as in the examples above. However, when **bù** is followed by a verb with Tone 4, it needs to be changed to **bú**. Examples:

bú shì	not be
bú jiào	not called
bú qù	not go

Helpful Tip: When Yě is Used with Bù

Yě needs to precede **bù** as in the sentence: **Wǒ yě bù zhīdào.** ("I do not know, either.") More examples:

Wǒde Zhōngwén yě bù hǎo.	My Chinese is not good, either.
Yùndòng zhōngxīn jīntiān yě bù kāi.	The sports center is not open today, either.

GRAMMAR NOTE The Word **Kéyi** = "Can; May"

The auxiliary verb **kéyi** needs to be put between a subject and a verb. It is often used when a suggestion or a request is involved. Examples:

Nǐ kéyi shàngwǎng kàn yíxià.	You can take a look on the Internet.
Wǒ kéyi qǐng wèn nín yíge wèntí ma?	Could I ask you a question?
Wǒmen míngtiān kéyi yìqǐ dǎ lánqiú.	We can play basketball together tomorrow.

GRAMMAR NOTE Using **Yíxià** = "A While" To Soften the Verb

When **yíxià** is paired with a verb, the sentence becomes more polite and less abrupt, i.e., **Nǐ kéyi shàngwǎng kàn yíxià** sounds softer and more polite than **Nǐ kéyi shàngwǎng kàn.** Other examples:

Qù yíxià	go for a short while
Wèn yíxià	ask a quick (question)
Zuò yíxià	sit a while

CULTURAL NOTE Days of a Week

The formation of terms for the days of the week in Chinese is "**xīngqī** + number" except for Sunday. For Sunday, you should say **xīngqītiān** or the other rather formal term **xīngqīrì**. The term **xīngqī** can be replaced with **lǐbài**:

Xīngqīyī or lǐbàiyī	Monday
Xīngqī'èr or lǐbài'èr	Tuesday
Xīngqīsān or lǐbàisān	Wednesday
Xīngqīsì or lǐbàisì	Thursday
Xīngqīwǔ or lǐbàiwǔ	Friday
Xīngqīliù or lǐbàiliù	Saturday
Xīngqītiān or lǐbàitiān	Sunday
Xīngqīrì or lǐbàirì	Sunday (a little more formal)
Xīngqījǐ or lǐbàijǐ	Which day of the week

Pattern Practice 1

Practice saying the following phrases.
Noun 1 + **de** + noun 2

Wǒ de Zhōngwén míngzi	my Chinese name
Nǐ de xuéxiào	your school
Zhāng Lǎoshī de bàngōngshì	Professor Zhang's office
Xuéxiào de shítáng	the school's dining hall

Pattern Practice 2

Practice saying the following phrases.
Subject + **zài** + place word

Gāo Zhì'ān zài nǎr?	Where is Gao Zhi'an?
Wáng Mǐn zài kāfēidiàn.	Wang Min is at the coffee shop.
Wèishēngjiān zài pángbiān.	The restroom is on the side.
Tāde bàngōngshì zài duìmiàn.	His/Her office is right across.

Pattern Practice 3

Practice saying the following phrases.
Subject + **bù/bú** + verb phrase

Wǒ bú shì Měiguó rén.	I am not American.
Wǒ míngtiān bú qù túshūguǎn.	I am not going to the library tomorrow.

Wǒde Zhōngwén bù hǎo.   My Chinese is not good.
Wǒ bù zhīdào tā shì něiguó rén.   I don't know which country he/she is
                                       from.

Wèishēngjiān bú zài túshūguǎnde   The restroom is not beside the library.
   pángbiān.

Pattern Practice 4

Practice saying the following phrases.
Subject + **kéyi** + verb phrase

Nǐ kéyi shàngwǎng kàn yíxià.   You can take a look on the Internet.
Wǒmen kéyi qù mǎi yìdiǎnr dōngxi.   We can go and buy a few things.
Wǒmen míngtiān kéyi yìqǐ yùndòng.   We can work out together tomorrow.
Wǒmen jīntiān kéyi yìqǐ qù yóuyǒng. We can go swim together today.

Pattern Practice 5

Verb + **yíxià**

Nǐ kéyi kàn yíxià.   You can take a look.
Nǐ kéyi qù yíxià.   You can go.
Nǐ kéyi wèn yíxià.   You can ask.
Nǐ kéyi zuò yíxià.   You can have a seat.

EXERCISE SET 1

Fill in each blank with one of the following expressions.

kéyi	yíxià	zài	yě

1. A: **Qǐng nǐ kàn** _____?
   B: **Hǎo.**

2. **Nǐ** _____ **shàngwǎng kàn yíxià yùndòng zhōngxīn míngtiān jǐdiǎn kāi?**

3. **Qǐng wèn, túshūguǎn** _____ **yùndòng zhōngxīnde duìmiàn ma?**

4. A: **Xiànzài jǐdiǎn?**
   B: **Wǒ** _____ **bù zhīdào.**

EXERCISE SET 2
Answer each of the following questions in Chinese.

1. **Nǐ xuéxiàode yóuyǒngguǎn zài nǎr?**
2. **Nǐ xuéxiàode yùndòng zhōngxīn zěnmeyàng?**
3. **Nǐ xīngqījǐ yùndòng?**
4. **Nǐ zài sùshè** (dorm room) **kéyi shàngwǎng ma?**

EXERCISE SET 3
Translate the following dialogues into Chinese.

1. A: Excuse me, where is the sports center?
   B: It's next to the library. Do you know where the library is?
   A: Yes, I do. Thank you.
   B: You are welcome.

2. A: What day is today?
   B: Today is Tuesday.
   A: Is the swimming complex open today?
   B: I don't know. You can take a look on the Internet.
   A: Okay.

3. A: Are you going to work today?
   B: Today is Saturday, so I am not going.
   A: Then let's go work out together. How about that?
   B: Great.

EXERCISE SET 4
Based on the sign, answer the following questions in Chinese.

```
                 Library Opening Hours
      Monday through Friday: 7 am to 11 pm
      Saturday: 8 am to 10 pm
      Sunday: 8 am to 12 pm
```

1. **Túshūguǎn xīngqīyī jídiǎn kāi?**
2. **Túshūguǎn xīngqīliù jídiǎn kāi?**
3. **Túshūguǎn xīngqītiān xiàwǔ kāi ma?**

LESSON 8
Eating and Drinking

:::DIALOGUE::: Lunch Conversation

When Wang Min and Eric Goodman are having a casual conversation during lunch at the school's dining hall.

Min:	Gao Zhi'an, do you like Chinese food?
	Gāo Zhì'ān, nǐ xǐhuan chī Zhōngguó cài ma?
	高志安，你喜欢吃中国菜吗？
Eric:	I like it very much. I especially like the spicy Chinese dishes.
	Wǒ hěn xǐhuan, wǒ tèbié xǐhuan chī làde Zhōngguó cài.
	我很喜欢，我特别喜欢吃辣的中国菜。
Min:	Where do you usually eat?
	Nǐ píngcháng zài nǎr chīfàn?
	你平常在哪儿吃饭？
Eric:	Sometimes I eat at the school's dining halls, and sometimes I go to the restaurants outside.
	Yǒude shíhou zài xuéxiàode shítáng, yǒude shíhou qù wàimiànde cānguǎn.
	有的时候在学校的食堂，有的时候去外面的餐馆。
Min:	How do you feel about the food at the school's dining halls?
	Nǐ juéde xuéxiào shítángde cài zěnmeyàng?
	你觉得学校食堂的菜怎么样？
Eric:	It's cheap and also tasty. But sometimes it is too oily.
	Hěn piányi, yě hěn hǎochī, kěshi yǒude shíhou tài yóu le.
	很便宜，也很好吃，可是有的时候太油了。

New Vocabulary

Pinyin	Chinese Character	English
Xǐhuan	喜欢	Like
Chī	吃	Eat
Cài	菜	Food, dish (lit., vegetables)
Hěn	很	Very, very much
Tèbié	特别	Especially, special
Là	辣	Spicy
Píngcháng	平常	Usually
Zài	在	Be located at
Chīfàn	吃饭	Dine, eat food
Yǒude shíhou	有的时候	Sometimes
Wàimiàn	外面	Outside
Cānguǎn	餐馆	Restaurant

New Vocabulary (cont'd)

Pinyin	Chinese Character	English
Juéde	觉得	Feel, think
Piányi	便宜	Cheap, inexpensive
Hǎochī	好吃	Good tasting, tasty, delicious
Kěshi	可是	But
Tài...le	太...了	Too...
Yóu	油	Greasy, oily

Supplementary Vocabulary Flavor Stative Verbs

Pinyin	English
kǔ	bitter
suān	sour
tàng	hot (temperature)
tián	sweet, sugary
xián	salty

Stative Verb Pairs

Pinyin	English
Duō vs. **shǎo**	Much vs. little
Piányi vs. **guì**	Cheap vs. expensive
Hǎochī vs. **nánchī**	Delicious vs. awful (to eat)

Frequency Adverbs

Pinyin	English
Bùcháng	Not often
Chángcháng	Often
Hěn shǎo	Rarely; seldom
Zǒngshì	Always

GRAMMAR NOTE   The Word **Xǐhuan** = "Like"

The verb **xǐhuan**, which indicates one's preference for something, can be followed either by a verb phrase or by a noun. Examples:

xǐhuan dǎ lánqiú	like to play basketball
xǐhuan shàngwǎng	like to surf the Internet
xǐhuan yùndòng	like to exercise
xǐhuan Zhōngguó cài	like Chinese food
xǐhuan Zhōngguó lìshǐ	like Chinese history

To negate, use **bú tài xǐhuan** instead of **bù xǐhuan**. Although both are grammatical, **bú tài xǐhuan** is more polite than the more straightforward **bù xǐhuan**.

Examples:

Wǒ bú tài xǐhuan làde cài.   I don't really like spicy food.
Wǒ bú tài xǐhuan yùndòng.   I don't really like to exercise.

GRAMMAR NOTE   The Word **Cài** = "Food, Dish"

The term **cài** can refer to food in general or an individual dish. Examples:

Zhōngguó cài	Chinese food
Měiguó cài	American food
suānde cài	sour dishes
làde cài	spicy dishes

GRAMMAR NOTE   Using the Adverb **Hěn** = "Very" as Intensifier

There are two important usages of the adverb **hěn**. One is "Subject + **hěn** + verb phrase." **Hěn** in this case serves as a degree intensifier meaning "very" or "very much." Examples:

Wǒ hěn xǐhuan Zhōngguó cài.   I like Chinese food very much.
Wǒ hěn xǐhuan yùndòng.   I like to exercise very much.
Wǒ hěn xiǎng qù Zhōngguó.   I want to go to China very much.

The other usages of **hěn** is "Subject + **hěn** + stative verb." **Hěn** in this case does not mean "very" unless it is stressed; it merely functions as a grammatical marker.

Examples of this use of **hěn**:

Shítángde cài hěn piányi.   The food in the dining hall is cheap.
Nǐde Zhōngwén hěn hǎo.   Your Chinese is good.
Gāo Zhì'ān hěn kèqi.   Gao Zhi'an is polite.

Remember, it is incorrect to say:

Shítángde cài piányi.
Nǐde Zhōngwén hǎo.
Gāo Zhì'ān kèqi.

GRAMMAR NOTE   The Word **Zài** = "Be Located at"

You have learned **zài** as a verb in Lesson 7. In this lesson, **zài** is a coverb that is typically used in the structure "Subject + **zài** + Place + Verb phrase." Examples:

Nǐ píngcháng zài nǎr chīfàn?	Where do you usually eat?
Wǒ xǐhuan zài yùndòng zhōngxīn yùndòng.	I like to exercise at the sports center.
Gāo Zhì'ān chángcháng zài wàimiànde cānguǎn chīfàn.	Gao Zhi'an often dines in the restaurants (away from campus).

Helpful Tip:

A location phrase (e.g. **zài** + Place) in Chinese needs to be put between the subject and the main verb in a sentence. It is wrong to say **Zài nǎr nǐ píngcháng chīfàn** or **Nǐ píngcháng chīfàn zài nǎr**.

GRAMMAR NOTE   Using Frequency Adverbs **Píngcháng** = "Often" and **Yǒude Shíhou** = "Occasionally"

You learn several frequency adverbs in this lesson, such as **píngcháng**, **yǒude shíhou**, and others in the supplementary vocabulary. Frequency adverbs should be placed between the subject and the verb phrase. Although **píngcháng** and **yǒude shíhou** can also appear in the beginning of a sentence, we encourage you to put them after the subject. Examples:

Nǐ píngcháng zài nǎr chīfàn?	Where do you usually eat?
Wǒ bù cháng yùndòng.	I don't exercise often.
Gāo Zhì'ān yǒude shíhou zài xuéxiàode shítáng chīfàn.	Sometimes Gao Zhi'an eats at the school's dining hall.

GRAMMAR NOTE   Using **Juéde** = To "Feel, Think" to Elicit Opinions

Juéde is a good verb to elicit thoughts and opinions and is usually paired with **zěnmeyàng** (see Lesson 6). Examples:

Nǐ juéde Zhōngguó cài zěnmeyàng?	How do you feel about Chinese food?
Wǒ juéde shítángde cài tài yóu le.	I think our dining hall's food is too greasy.
Nǐ juéde xuéxiàode yùndòng zhōngxīn zěnmeyàng?	What do you think about our school's sports center?

GRAMMAR NOTE "And" Omitted to Connect Two Sentences

Pay attention to the structure of **Hěn piányi, yě hěn hǎochī.** You don't need a conjunction word "and" to connect **hěn piányi** and **hěn hǎochī. Yě** means "also" and it goes before the verb and after the subject. More examples:

Wǒ shì Měiguó rén, tā shì Zhōngguó rén.	I am American and he/she is Chinese.
Wǒ xǐhuan chī làde cài, tā xǐhuan chī suānde cài.	I like spicy food and he/she likes sour food.

GRAMMAR NOTE Using The Conjunction Word **Kěshi** = "But" to Show Differing Opinions

You have learned your first conjunction word **suóyi** "so" in Lesson 7. In this lesson, you learn **kěshi** to show contrast or express different opinions. **Kěshi** can connect two sentences or verb phrases, but not nouns. Examples:

Xuéxiào shítángde cài hěn piányi, kěshi tài yóule.	The food in the school's dining hall is cheap, but it's too greasy.
Gāo Zhì'ān píngcháng xǐhuan chī Zhōngguó cài, kěshi tā jīntiān chī Rìběn cài.	Gao Zhi'an usually likes to eat Chinese food, but today he is eating Japanese food.
Lǐ Yáng zǒngshì hěn máng, kěshi tā jīntiān bù máng.	Li Yang is always busy, but today he is not.

GRAMMAR NOTE Using The Phrase **Tài ... le** = "Too..." as Intensifier

You use **tài** + Stative Verb + **le** to express extreme degrees. Examples:

tài piányile	too cheap
tài hǎochīle	so tasty
tài tiánle	too sweet

To negate, you add **bú** before **tài** and drop the **le** at the end:

bú tài piányi	not too cheap
bú tài hǎochī	not so tasty
bú tài tián	not too sweet

Do not combine "**tài** + Stative Verb + **le**" with **hěn.** It is ungrammatical to say **hěn tài piányile** "very too cheap already".

CULTURAL NOTE — Using **Bú Tài** + Stative Verb = "Not Too ..." to Soften Negative Meanings

When the stative verb has a negative meaning, Chinese people tend not to use the "**tài** + Stative Verb + **le**" structure unless they are friends and know each other well. Instead, they used the "**bú tài** + Stative Verb" structure. Instead of saying:

Shítángde cài tài nánchīle.	The food in the dining hall is awful.
Wàimiànde dōngxi tài guìle.	The things outside are too expensive.

You say:

Shítángde cài bú tài hǎochī.	The food in the dining hall is not so tasty.
Wàimiànde dōngxi bú tài piányi.	The things outside are not so cheap.

Excessive use of the "**tài** + **stative verb** + **le**" structure may run the risk of being considered judgmental or arrogant, as the Chinese culture appreciates indirect expressions of opinions in formal conversation. In this dialogue, Eric Goodman uses this structure because he knows Wang Min and they are both students. Their interaction is rather informal.

Pattern Practice 1

Practice saying the following phrases.
Subject + **xǐhuan**

Wǒ xǐhuan Zhōngguó lìshǐ.	I like Chinese history.
Wǒ xǐhuan wǒde Zhōngwén míngzi.	I like my Chinese name.
Wǒ xǐhuan xué Zhōngwén.	I like learning the Chinese language.
Wǒ xǐhuan chī Zhōngguó cài.	I like to eat Chinese food.
Wǒ xǐhuan qù yùndòng zhōngxīn dǎ lánqiú.	I like to go to the sports center to play basketball.

Pattern Practice 2

Practice saying the following phrases.
Subject + **hěn** + stative verb

Wǒ hěn máng.	I am busy.
Zhōngwén hěn nán.	Chinese is difficult.
Nǐde Yīngyǔ hěn hǎo.	Your English is good.
Wàimiànde cānguǎn hěn guì.	The restaurants outside are expensive.

Pattern Practice 3

Practice saying the following phrases.
Subject + **zài** + place + verb phrase

Wǒ píngcháng zài shítáng chīfàn.	I usually eat at the dining hall.
Wáng Mǐn zài shāngdiàn mǎi dōngxi.	Wang Min is buying things at a store.
Lǐ Yáng zài yùndòng zhōngxīn yùndòng.	Li Yang is working out at the sports center.
Gāo Zhì'ān zài Qīnghuá Dàxué xué Zhōngwén.	Gao Zhi'an is learning Chinese at Tsinghua University.

Pattern Practice 4

Practice saying the following phrases.
Subject + frequency adverb + verb phrase

Wǒ chángcháng yùndòng.	I often exercise.
Wǒ hěn shǎo chī làde cài.	I seldom eat spicy food.
Wǒ zǒngshì qù shūdiàn.	I always go to the bookstore
Wǒ píngcháng zài shítáng chīfàn.	I usually eat at the dining hall.

Pattern Practice 5

Practice saying the following phrases.

Subject + **tài** + stative verb + **le**

Tā tài mángle.	He/She is too busy.
Wǒmen xuéxiào shítángde cài tài piányile.	The food in our school's dining hall is so cheap.
Wǒmen xuéxiào shítángde cài tài hǎochīle.	The food in our school's dining hall is so tasty.
Wàimiàn cānguǎnde cài tài yóule.	The food in the restaurants outside is too greasy.

Pattern Practice 6

Practice saying the following phrases.

Subject + **bú tài** + stative verb

Wǒde Zhōngwén bú tài hǎo.	My Chinese is not so good.
Wàimiàn cānguǎnde cài bú tài piányi.	The food in the restaurants outside is not so cheap.
Wǒmen xuéxiào shítángde cài bú tài hǎochī.	The food in our school's dining hall is not so tasty.

EXERCISE 1

Fill in each blank with one of the following expressions.

juéde	tài	kěshi	yě

1. **Jīntiānde cài _____ làle.**

2. **Yóuyǒngguǎn píngcháng jiǔdiǎn kāi, _____ jīntiān shíyīdiǎn kāi.**

3. **Wǒ hěn xǐhuan chī Zhōngguó cài, tā _____ hěn xǐhuan.**

4. **Nǐ _____ xuéxiào shítángde cài zěnmeyàng?**

EXERCISE 2

Answer each of the following questions in Chinese.

1. **Nǐ xǐhuan chī něiguó cài?**
2. **Nǐ píngcháng zài nǎr chīfàn?**
3. **Nǐ chángcháng qù wàimiànde cānguǎn chīfàn ma?**
4. **Nǐ xuéxiào shítángde cài zěnmeyàng?**

EXERCISE 3

Translate the following dialogues into Chinese.

1. A: Do you like Chinese food?
   B: I do. I also like Thai food. Do you like spicy food?
   A: I don't like it that much.

2. A: Where do you usually eat?
   B: I usually eat at the dining hall.
   A: How do you think about the food in the dining hall?
   B: It's not expensive, and it is tasty.

3. A: What kind of food do you like?
   B: Sometimes I like spicy food, and sometimes I like sour food. How about you?
   A: I like tasty food.

EXERCISE 4

Role Play

You are chatting with your Chinese friend about food. You are curious about the following questions: (1) Where does he/she usually eat? (2) What is the food in his/her dining hall like? (3) What kind of food does he/she like or dislike?

LESSON 9
Going Shopping

▢ DIALOGUE ▢ Buying Clothes

Eric Goodman is buying clothes at a shopping mall in Beijing.

Eric:	Excuse me, do you have the medium size for this shirt/dress?
	Qǐng wèn, zhèijiàn yīfu yǒu-méiyou zhōnghàode?
	请问,这件衣服有没有中号的?
Salesperson:	Yes, would you like to try it on?
	Yǒu, nǐ yào-búyào shìchuān yíxià?
	有,你要不要试穿一下?
Eric:	Yes. Can I also try on that large one?
	Hǎo, wǒ kéyi-bùkéyi yě shìchuān nèijiàn dàhàode?
	好,我可以不可以也试穿那件大号的?
Salesperson:	Of course you can. Does the size fit?
	Dāngrán kéyi. Dàxiǎo zěnmeyàng?
	当然可以。大小怎么样?
Eric:	The medium size fits better. I will buy the medium size one.
	Zhōnghàode bǐjiào héshì, wǒ mǎi zhōnghàode.
	中号的比较合适,我买中号的。
Salesperson:	Okay. Would you like to pay in cash or with a credit card?
	Hǎo, nǐ fùxiàn háishì shuākǎ?
	好,你付现还是刷卡?
Eric:	With my credit card.
	Wǒ shuākǎ.
	我刷卡。

New Vocabulary

Pinyin	Chinese Character	English
Qǐng wèn	请问	Excuse me, may I ask
Zhèi-	这	This
Jiàn	件	(Measure word for clothes)
Yīfu	衣服	Collective word for clothes; can also mean a single garment like a shirt or dress
Méiyou	没有	Do not have, there is/are no
Zhōnghào	中号	Medium size, medium
Yào	要	Want to
Shìchuān	试穿	Try on (lit., try wear)
Nèi-	那	That
Dàhào	大号	Large size (dà "big, large")
Dāngrán	当然	Of course

New Vocabulary (cont'd)

Pinyin	Chinese Character	English
Xiǎo	小	Small, little
Dàxiǎo	大小	Size
Bǐjiào	比较	Comparatively, relatively
Héshì	合适	Suitable, fitting
Fùxiàn	付现	Pay in cash (**xiànjīn** "cash" and **fù** "pay")
Háishì	还是	Or, also means "still"
Shuākǎ	刷卡	Pay with credit card; (**xìngyòngkǎ** "credit card," **shuā** "swipe")

Supplementary Vocabulary

Clothes that are Used with the Measure Word -**Jiàn**

Pinyin	English
Chènyī	Shirt
Kùzi	Pants
Tǐxùshān	T-shirt
Wàitào	Jacket

GRAMMAR NOTE

Using **Zhèi**, **Nèi** "This, That" To Identify the Noun

The **zhèi/nèi** (this/that) in the pattern "**zhèi/nèi** + Measure Word + Noun" serves as a specifier to clearly identify the noun. Examples:

Zhèige cānguǎnde cài hěn hǎochī.	The food in this restaurant is tasty.
Wǒ hěn xǐhuan nèige kāfēidiàn.	I like that coffee shop very much.
Zhèijiàn yīfu dàxiǎo héshì ma?	Does this shirt/dress fit?

People in the southern part of China tend to say **zhè** instead of **zhèi** and **nà** instead of **nèi**. Either version would work just fine.

GRAMMAR NOTE ## The Word **Méiyou** = "Not have, There is/ are no"

Unlike other verbs, the negation of **yǒu** (have) is **méiyou**, not **bùyou**. Note that the tone of **yǒu** is neutralized in its negation form **méiyou**. Examples:

Zhèijiàn yīfu méiyou zhōnghàode.	There is no medium size for this shirt/ dress.
Wǒmende xuéxiào méiyou yóuyǒngguǎn.	There is no swimming complex in our school.
Wǒ méiyou wèntí.	I don't have any questions/problems.

GRAMMAR NOTE ## Using Affirmative + Negative to Form a Yes–No Question

In Lesson 4, you learned the structure "Statement + **ma**" to form a simple Yes–No question in Chinese. In this lesson, you learn the other question form: Affirmative + Negative. Examples of these question forms include: **shì-búshì** "Is, is not", **yǒu-méiyou** "Have, have not", and **kāi-bùkāi** "Open, not open". Examples:

Statement:

Nǐ shì xuésheng.	You are a student.
Tā yǒu shìr.	He/She has things to do.
Yóuyǒngguǎn jīntiān kāi.	The swimming complex is open today.

Questions with **ma**:

Nǐ shì xuésheng ma?	Are you a student?
Tā yǒu shìr ma?	Does he/she have things to do?
Yóuyǒngguǎn jīntiān kāi ma?	Is the swimming complex open today?

Questions with "Affirmative + Negative" structure:

Nǐ shì-búshì xuésheng?	Are you a student?
Tā yǒu-méiyou shìr?	Does he/she have things to do?
Yóuyǒngguǎn jīntiān kāi-bùkāi?	Is the swimming complex open today?

Do not combine the "Statement + **ma**" and the "Affirmative + Negative" to form a question.

GRAMMAR NOTE **Using the Word -De = "Belonging to, Of" to Nominalize Phrase**

In the sentence **zhèijiàn yīfu yǒu-méiyou zhōnghàode** ("Do you have a medium size for this shirt/dress?") it's clear that **zhōnghàode** refers to the clothing and thus we can omit the words **yīfu** after **zhōnghàode**. Examples:

Zhèijiàn yīfu yǒu-méiyou dàhàode?	Do you have the large size for this?
Wǒ xǐhuan chī làde.	I like to eat spicy (food).
Nǐ yào-búyào shìchuān yíxià zhōnghàode?	Do you want to try on the medium size one?

The context is clear from the words **shìchuān** "try", **yīfu** "clothes" and **chī** "to eat", thus the subjects of the sentences must be a shirt or dress for the first two examples, and food for the third.

GRAMMAR NOTE **Using the Topic + Comment Structure**

Together with the "Subject + verb + object" structure you have learned, the "Topic + comment" is the other structure widely used in Chinese, especially when the topic is clear for both interlocutors from the context. The topic is usually a noun specified by the speaker and the comment is usually a verb phrase or a sentence. Examples:

Topic + Comment (verb phrase)

Zhèige cài tài yóule.	This dish is too greasy.
Nèige cānguǎn zěnmeyàng?	How is that restaurant?

Topic + Comment (sentence)

Nèijiàn kùzi wǒ mǎi dàhàode.	I will buy the large size for that pair of pants.
Zhèijiàn chènyī wǒ shuākǎ.	I will pay for this shirt with my credit card.
Xuéxiào shítángde cài wǒ bú tài xǐhuan.	I don't really like the food at the school's dining hall.

GRAMMAR NOTE **Using the Word Yào = "Want to"**

Yào means "want to" and it needs to be placed between the subject and the verb phrase. Examples:

Nǐ yào-búyào shìchuān yíxià?	Do you want to try it on?
Nǐ yào yìqǐ qù chīfàn ma?	Do you want to eat together?
Nǐ míngtiān yào-búyào yìqǐ dǎ lánqiú?	Do you want to play basketball together tomorrow?

Compared to the **xiǎng** (would like to) you learned in Lesson 5, **yào** is more casual. We suggest you use **xiǎng** when you speak with someone older and of higher social status and **yào** for your friends.

GRAMMAR NOTE The Word **Bǐjiào** = "Comparatively, Relatively"

Subject + **bǐjiào** + stative verb expresses comparison. Examples:

Míngtiān bǐjiào hǎo.	Tomorrow is better.
Zhèijiàn tǐxùshān bǐjiào héshì.	This t-shirt fits better.
Xuéxiào shítángde cài bǐjiào piányi.	The food in the school's dining hall is cheaper.

GRAMMAR NOTE Using the Word **Háishì** = "Or" for Options

Háishì can be inserted between two verb phrases or nouns to inquire about preferences or opinions. Examples:

Jīntiān shì xīngqīliù háishì xīngqītiān?	Is today Saturday or Sunday?
Nǐ xǐhuan chī làde háishì suānde?	Do you like spicy or sour food?
Nǐ fùxiàn háishì shuākǎ?	Would you like to pay in cash or with a credit card?

Helpful Tip:
Háishì is used only in a question form; it cannot be used in a statement (e.g. Sunday or Sunday works for me).

CULTURAL NOTE Using the Word **Qǐng wèn** = "May I Ask"

This idiomatic expression **qǐng wèn** is used before a question or a request to mean "may I ask" or "excuse me." **Qǐng wèn** is a sophisticated way to initiate a question or ask for a favor from strangers or acquaintances. It is rarely used between friends. Examples:

Qǐng wèn, xiànzài jǐdiǎn?	Excuse me, what time is it?
Qǐng wèn, yùndòng zhōngxīn jīntiān kāi ma?	Excuse me, is the sports center open today?

CULTURAL NOTE Ways of Payment

Fùxiàn and **shuākǎ** are two ways of payment in China. In general, smaller stores or street vendors still prefer cash though more and more shops accept credit cards. The term **fùxiàn** is composed of **fù** (to pay) and **xiàn** (short for **xiànjīn** or "cash") **while shuākǎ** is composed of **shuā** (to swipe) and **kǎ** (short for **xìnyòng-kǎ** or "credit card"). Both terms are used as verbs in Chinese.

Pattern Practice 1

Practice saying the following phrases.
Zhèi/Nèi (This/That) + measure word + noun

Zhèige cānguǎn	This restaurant
Zhèige shítáng	This dining hall
Zhèijiàn yīfu	This shirt/dress
Nèijiàn kùzi	That pants
Nèige wèntí	That question

Pattern Practice 2

Practice saying the following phrases.
Affirmative + Negative to form a Yes–No question

Nǐ máng-bùmáng?	Are you busy?
Zhōngwén nán-bùnán?	Is Chinese difficult?
Jīntiānde cài hǎochī-bùhǎochī?	Is the food today tasty?
Nǐ yào-búyào qù chīfàn?	Do you want to go and eat?
Zhèijiàn tīxùshān yǒu-méiyou zhōnghàode?	Do you have this T-shirt in a medium size?

Pattern Practice 3

Practice saying the following phrases.

Topic + Comment (verb phrase)

Nèige cài tài làle.	That dish is too spicy.
Zhèijiàn yīfu tài xiǎole.	This shirt/dress is too small.
Fùxiàn bǐjiào piányi.	It's cheaper to pay in cash.

Topic + Comment (sentence)

Nèijiàn kùzi wǒ bú tài xǐhuan.	I don't really like that pair of pants.
Làde cài Gāo Zhì'ān tèbié xǐhuan.	Gao Zhi'an really likes spicy food.
Zhōnghàode wàitào tāmen méiyou.	They don't have any medium-sized jackets.

Pattern Practice 4

Practice saying the following phrases.
Subject + **yào** + verb phrase

Nǐ yào yìqǐ qù mǎi yīfu ma?	Do you want to go buy clothes together?
Nǐ yào yìqǐ qù chīfàn ma?	Do you want to go eat together?
Nǐ yào fùxiàn háishì shuākǎ?	Do you want to pay by cash or credit card?
Wǒ míngtiān yào qù yùndòng zhōngxīn.	I want to go to the sports center tomorrow.

Pattern Practice 5

Practice saying the following phrases.
Subject + **bǐjiào** + stative verb

Nèige cānguǎnde cài bǐjiào hǎochī.	The food in that restaurant tastes better.
Xuéxiào shítángde cài bǐjiào piányi.	The food in the school's dining hall is cheaper.
Tāmende dōngxi bǐjiào guì.	Their things are more expensive.
Wǒ jīntiān bǐjiào máng.	I am busier today.

Pattern Practice 6

Practice saying the following phrases.
Use **háishì** between two noun phrases or verb phrases to inquire about preferences or which person the conversation is about.

Lǐ Yáng háishì Wáng Mǐn?	Li Yang or Wang Min?
Míngtiān xiàwǔ sìdiǎn háishì wǔdiǎn?	Tomorrow at 4 pm or 5 pm?
Tā shì Měiguó rén háishì Zhōngguó rén?	Is he/she American or Chinese?

Chinese or American?

Nǐ fùxiàn háishì shuākǎ?	Would you like to pay in cash or with a credit card?
Nǐ yào shìchuān zhōnghàode háishì dàhàode?	Do you want to try the medium or the large one?

EXERCISE 1

Fill in each blank with one of the following expressions.

kéyi	dàxiǎo	héshì	háishì

1. **Zhèijiàn yīfude** _____ **zěnmeyàng?**

2. **Nèijiàn kùzi** _____ **ma?**

3. **Qǐng wèn, wǒ** _____ **shìchuān yīxià zhèijiàn tīxùshān ma?**

4. A: **Nǐ fùxiàn** _____ **shuākǎ?**
   B: **Wǒ fùxiàn.**

EXERCISE 2

Answer each of the following questions in Chinese.

1. **Nǐ píngcháng xǐhuan qù nǎr mǎi yīfu?**
2. **Nǐ chuān dàhàode, zhōnghàode, háishì xiǎohàode yīfu?**
3. **Nǐ xǐhuan fùxiàn háishì shuākǎ?**

EXERCISE 3

Translate the following dialogues into Chinese.

1. A: Excuse me, do you have the small size for these pants?
   B: Yes. Would you like to try it on?
   A: Yes.

2. A: Which one fits better? The large one or the medium size one?
   B: The large one fits better. I shall buy the large one.
   A: Okay.

3. A: How is the size?
   B: It fits well. Can I use credit cards?
   A: Of course you can.

EXERCISE 4

Role Play

You are shopping at a clothing store in Shanghai. Ask the store clerk the following questions: (1) Can you try on the pants? (2) Do they have the large size of the pants? (3) Can you use credit cards?

Credit card payments are a norm in China.

LESSON 10

Introduction to the Chinese Writing System (I)

The official writing system of Chinese language comprises characters. A character is called **zì** (literally "word") in Chinese, so Chinese characters are called **Zhōngguó zì** or **Hànzì**. Each character corresponds to one syllable. For example, the term **Zhōngguó** (China) has two syllables (**Zhōng** and **guó**), so it contains two characters. Zhōng is written as 中, **guó** is written as 国, so **Zhōngguó** is written as 中国.

The earliest set of Chinese characters in comparatively full forms dates back to 1200–1500 BC and was written on oracle bones. These characters are called **Jiǎgǔwén** (oracle bone inscriptions). Since then, Chinese characters have gone through a few significant evolutions in form. The characters used today are based on **Kǎishū** (Regular Script), the script that has served as the standard for writing since the end of Han Dynasty (206 BC–220 AD).

There are six ways of forming Chinese characters:

	Formation	English	Examples and Explanations
1.	**Xiàngxíngzì**	Pictographs	日 **rì** (sun) 川 **chuān** (river) The shape of the character 日 resembles the sun. Similarly, 川 resembles a river.
2.	**Zhǐshìzì**	Simple Ideographs	二 **èr** (two) – two lines represent "two." 中 **zhōng** (middle) – the line in the middle reveals the meaning of the character.
3.	**Huìyìzì**	Compound Ideographs	休 **xiū** (rest) 森 **sēn** (forest) The left component of 休 means "person" or 人 and the right component 木 means "wood." So 休 can be understood as "a person leaning next to a tree," or "to rest." When this character for wood is written thrice, as in 森, this forms a "forest".

Formation	English	Examples and Explanations
4. **Xíngshēngzì**	Semantic-Phonetic Compounds	饭 **fàn** (food) 请 **qǐng** (invite) A **Xíngshēngzì** consists of a semantic component and a phonetic component. The semantic component, usually on the lefthand side, reveals the meaning or category of the character. The phonetic component, usually on the right-hand side, gives you a hint of the sound of the character. The left component 饣 of 饭 means it is "food-related." The right component 反 is pronounced as **fǎn**, which sounds similar to the character 饭 **fàn**. Similarly, the left component 讠 of 请 indicates it is "speech-related." The right component 青 is pronounced as **qīng**, which sounds similar to the character 请 **qǐng**.
5. **Zhuǎnzhùzì**	Mutually Explanatory Characters	考 **kǎo** (test) 老 **lǎo** (old) These two characters are similar in form, sounds, and meanings. **Zhuǎnzhùzì** are smallest in percentage in Chinese characters.
6. **Jiǎjièzì**	Borrowed Characters	令 **lìng** (command) 长 **zhǎng** (the elderly) The original meaning of 令 is "command." Later it is borrowed to form other compounds such as 县令 (**xiànlìng** "county magistrate"). Similarly, the original meaning of 长 is "the elderly." Later it is borrowed to form other compounds such as 县长 (**xiànzhǎng** "county's head commissioner").

Some learners of Chinese are surprised to find that the majority of Chinese characters are **Xíngshēngzì**, not **Xiàngxíngzì**. That means most Chinese characters are not pictures; instead, they are composed of one semantic component and one phonetic component. The semantic component refers to the meaning or category of the character while the phonetic component reveals what the character may sound like.

Scholars have not come to a conclusion about the total number of Chinese characters, but the most authoritative dictionaries include about 50,000. This number may seem intimidating to learn, but the good news is that the most commonly used characters actually amount to less than 4,000 of these 50,000. As a matter of fact, if you know 1,000 to 1,500 characters, you can already read simple Chinese stories. Being able to recognize 2,500 to 3,000 characters will enable you to read Chinese newspapers and common books.

In this book we will introduce 25 characters each in Lesson 10 and Lesson 20. These 50 characters are commonly seen on a daily basis while you work or travel in China. If you plan to continue your study of the Chinese written language, we encourage you to explore other related books published by Tuttle.

Character	Pinyin	English	Compounds
一	yī	one	
二	èr	two	
三	sān	three	
四	sì	four	
五	wǔ	five	
六	liù	six	
七	qī	seven	
八	bā	eight	
九	jiǔ	nine	
十	shí	ten	九十 **jiǔshí** (ninety)
百	bǎi	hundred	三百 **sānbǎi** (three hundred)
千	qiān	thousand	八千 **bāqiān** (eight thousand)
元	yuán	dollar	五百元 **wǔbǎi yuán** (five hundred dollars)
是	shì	be	
你	nǐ	you	你是… **nǐ shì…** (You are…)
我	wǒ	I, me	我是… **wǒ shì…** (I am…)
他	tā	he, him	他是… **tā shì…** (He is…)

Character	Pinyin	English	Compounds
她	tā	she, her	她是… **tā shì…** (She is…)
谢	xiè	thank	谢谢 **xièxie** (thank you) The second 谢 loses its tone in the compound 谢谢.
国	guó	nation, country	
中	zhōng	middle	中国 **Zhōngguó** (China)
美	měi	pretty, beautiful	美国 **Měiguó** (U.S.A.)
人	rén	people	中国人 **Zhōngguó rén** (Chinese people) 美国人 **Měiguó rén** (American people)
岁	suì	years of age	二十岁 **èrshí suì** (twenty years old)
好	hǎo	good	你好 **nǐ hǎo** (Hi)

EXERCISE
Practice reading the following sentences.

1. 你好，我是 Eric。
   Nǐ hǎo, wǒ shì Eric.
   Hi, I am Eric.

2. 我二十岁。
   Wǒ èrshí suì.
   I am twenty years old.

3. 我是美国人，他是中国人。
   Wǒ shì Měiguó rén, tā shì Zhōngguó rén.
   I am American. He is Chinese.

4. 六百元。
   Liùbǎi yuán.
   Six hundred RMB.

5. 五千元。
   Wǔqiān yuán.
   Five thousand RMB.

6. 谢谢。
   Xièxie.
   Thank you.

LESSON 11
Making a Phone Call

DIALOGUE Calling Manager Lin

Manager Lin and Eric Goodman met at a career fair on campus. Manager Lin asked if Eric would be interested in working for him. After days of consideration Eric is calling Manager Lin. Manager Lin's office assistant answers the phone.

Eric: Hello? May I speak with Manager Lin?
Wéi, nín hǎo, qǐng wèn, Lín Jīnglǐ zài ma?
喂，您好，请问，林经理在吗？

Assistant: The manager is not here right now. May I know who is speaking?
Jīnglǐ xiànzài bú zài. Qǐng wèn nín shì něiwèi?
经理现在不在。请问您是哪位？

Eric: My last name is Gao, and I am a student of Tsinghua University. Manager Lin asked me to call him.
Wǒ xìng Gāo, shì Qīnghuá Dàxuéde xuésheng. Lín Jīnglǐ yào wǒ gěi tā dǎ diànhuà.
我姓高，是清华大学的学生。林经理要我给他打电话。

Assistant: Okay, I will notify the manager and ask him to return your call. Your telephone number is …?
Hǎo, wǒ huì tōngzhī jīnglǐ, qǐng tā gěi nín huí diàn. Nínde diànhuà hàomǎ shì …?
好，我会通知经理，请他给您回电。您的电话号码是…？

Eric: My cell phone number is 139-2227-6688.
Wǒde shǒujī hàomǎ shì 139-2227-6688.
我的手机号码是 139-2227-6688。

Assistant: Great, Mr. Gao, I got it.
Hǎo, Gāo Xiānsheng, wǒ zhīdàole.
好，高先生，我知道了。

Eric: Thank you.
Xièxie.
谢谢。

Assistant: You are welcome.
Náli.
哪里。

New Vocabulary

Pinyin	Chinese Character	English
Wéi	喂	"Hello" (on the telephone)
Lín	林	Lin
Jīnglǐ	经理	Manager
Zài	在	Be present, around
Xiànzài	现在	Now
Wèi	位	(Polite measure word for people)
Xìng	姓	Be surnamed
Qīnghuá Dàxué	清华大学	Tsinghua University
Gěi	给	For, to
Diànhuà	电话	Telephone
Dǎ diànhuà	打电话	Make a phone call
Huì	会	Will
Tōngzhī	通知	Notify, inform
Huí diànhuà	回电话	Return a phone call
Hàomǎ	号码	Number (n)
Shǒujī	手机	Cellular phone or mobile phone
Yāo	1	One (used when reading out phone numbers)
Sān	3	Three
Jiǔ	9	Nine
Èr	2	Two
Qī	7	Seven
Liù	6	Six
Bā	8	Eight
Xiānsheng	先生	Mr.
Le	了	(Indicates change of state)
Nǎli	哪里	"You are welcome", "not at all", "it's nothing"

Supplementary Vocabulary Well-Established Chinese Universities

Pinyin	English
Běijīng Dàxué	Peking University, Beijing, Mainland China
Qīnghuá Dàxué	Tsinghua University, Beijing, Mainland China
Fùdàn Dàxué	Fudan University, Shanghai, Mainland China
Zhèjiāng Dàxué	Zhejiang University, Hangzhou, Mainland China
Táiwān Dàxué	Taiwan University, Taipei
Táiwān Shīfàn Dàxué	Taiwan Normal University, Taipei
Táiwān Qīnghuá Dàxué	Tsinghua University, Hsin-chu, Taiwan
Xiānggǎng Dàxué	The University of Hong Kong
Xiānggǎng Zhōngwén Dàxué	The Chinese University of Hong Kong

GRAMMAR NOTE The Word **Zài** = "Be Present"

You have learned **zài** as a verb to identify location in Lesson 7. Examples:

Wǒ zài shítáng.	I am in the dining hall.
Xuéxiàode yùndòng zhōngxīn zài nǎr?	Where is the sports center on campus?

You have also learned **zài** as a coverb in Lesson 8. Examples:

Nǐ píngcháng zài nǎr chīfàn?	Where do you usually eat?
Wǒ zài shāngdiàn mǎi dōngxi.	I am buying things at a store.

In this lesson, **zài** functions as a verb meaning "be present" to ask about someone's whereabouts. Examples:

Lín Jīnglǐ zài ma?	Is Manager Lin in?
Jīnglǐ xiànzài bú zài.	The manager is not here right now.

GRAMMAR NOTE The Word **Xìng** = "To be Surnamed"

Xìng is generally used as a verb in Chinese. Examples:

Wǒ xìng Gāo.	My last name is Gao.
Nèiwèi xiānsheng xìng Lín.	That gentleman's last name is Lin.

The most sophisticated way to inquire about someone's last name is **Nín guì xìng?** ("What is your honorable last name?"), not **nín xìng shénme**. **Nín guì xìng** is used on a rather formal occasion, such as in a business setting or in an international scholars' reception. Ask **nín guì xìng** so you can address people appropriately with heir titles (e.g., **Lín Jīnglǐ**, **Chén Xiānsheng**, or **Zhāng Lǎoshi**).

Helpful Tip:
(1) **Xìng** is followed by a last name only while **jiào** is followed by a full name. (2) **Nín guì xìng** is used in a formal occasion while **nǐ jiào shénme míngzi** is used in a more casual conversation.

GRAMMAR NOTE The Word **Gěi** as Coverb = "For" or "To"

Gěi as coverb often appears in the structure: Subject 1 + **gěi** + Subject 2 + verb phrase. Examples:

Wǒ gěi nǐ dǎ diànhuà.	I'll call you.
Wǒ qǐng tā gěi nín huí diàn.	I'll ask him to call you back.

Although structural variations with **gěi** as coverb exist, we encourage you to follow this pattern before a verb phrase.

GRAMMAR NOTE **The Diverse Meanings of the Verb Dǎ = "To Hit/Call"**

The verb **dǎ** has several meanings. In Lesson 6 we learned that **dǎ** as in **dǎ lánqiú** could mean "play basketball". In this lesson, **dǎ** means "call" and should be followed by **diànhuà** or **shǒujī**. Examples:

dǎ diànhuà	make a phone call
dǎ shǒujī	call cell phone

Helpful Tip:

If you want to say "call me", do not use **dǎ wǒ** which actually means "hit me". Instead, you should say **gěi wǒ dǎ diànhuà**.

GRAMMAR NOTE **The Auxiliary Verb Huì = "Will"**

The auxiliary verb **huì** means "will" and it indicates the potential realization of an action. Examples:

Wǒ huì tōngzhī jīnglǐ.	I will notify the manager.
Wǒ míngtiān huì qù yùndòng.	I will exercise tomorrow.
Nǐ jīntiān huì qù mǎi dōngxi ma?	Are you going to buy things today?

GRAMMAR NOTE **Using Le to Indicate a Change of Status**

The so-called sentence-final **le** indicates change of state. Compare:

Wǒ zhīdào.	I know. (as a response to **Nǐ zhīdào ma?**)
Wǒ zhīdàole.	Now I know. (I didn't know before. Now I know.)
Wǒmen yǒu zhōnghàode yīfu.	We have medium-sized shirts/dresses.
Wǒmen yǒu zhōnghàode yīfule.	Now we have medium-sized shirts/dresses. We didn't have them before. Now we do.
Wǒ yǒu Zhōngwén míngzi.	I have a Chinese name.
Wǒ yǒu Zhōngwén míngzile.	Now I have a Chinese name. I didn't have a Chinese name before. Now I do.

CULTURAL NOTE **Making and Answering a Phone Call**

When making or answering a phone call, Chinese people usually start with **wéi**. If you already know the caller or the receiver, **wéi** can be dropped and replaced with the terms of address for that person, such as **Gāo Zhì'ān**, **Lín Jīnglǐ**, or **Zhāng Lǎoshi**.

CULTURAL NOTE   Titles as Terms of Address

Note that the office assistant addresses Manager Lin as **jīnglǐ**. As mentioned in Lesson 5, it is common in Chinese culture to address people who are older and of higher social status simply with their titles, such as **xiānsheng** (Mr.), **lǎoshī** (teacher) and **jīnglǐ**.

CULTURAL NOTE   The Polite Measure Word **Wèi** to Refer to People (I)

You have learned **něi-** meaning "which" in Lesson 4, in phrases such as **Nǐ shì něiguó rén?** ("What country are you from?"). **Wèi** is a polite measure word for people, especially when they are present. So, **něiwèi** means "which person" and **zhèiwèi** means "this person."

If Eric Goodman and Li Yang meet Professor Zhang on campus, Eric can introduce them to each other by saying:

Zhāng Lǎoshi, nín hǎo, zhèiwèi shì wǒde péngyǒu, Lǐ Yáng. Lǐ Yáng, zhèiwèi shì Zhāng Lǎoshi.
Professor Zhang, how are you? This is my friend, Li Yang. Li Yang, this is Professor Zhang.

It would be inappropriate to use **ge** and say **Zhèige shì wǒde péngyǒu** or **Zhèige shì Zhāng Lǎoshi** as politeness is expected in this teacher-student scenario. Also, respect should be given to the elders and they should be introduced to the younger person first.

CULTURAL NOTE   Cell Phone Numbers in Mainland China

A typical cell phone number in Mainland China consists of 11 digits. It should be read by three digits + four digits + four digits. For instance, the cell phone number 13922276688 should be read as 139-2227-6688. Pausing at the wrong digit might hinder native speakers from jotting down the numbers.

CULTURAL NOTE   Response to **xièxie** "Thank you" is **Náli** "Not at all; it's Nothing"

Besides the **bié kèqi** or **bú kèqi** you learned in Lesson 5, **náli**, literally meaning "where" in the sense of "where does the gratitude come from," is another way to respond to **xièxie**.

Pattern Practice 1

Practice saying the following phrases.
Zài as verb

Gāo Zhì'ān zài.	Gao Zhi'an is here.
Lín Jīnglǐ zài ma?	Is Manager Lin in?
Lǐ Yáng xiànzài bú zài.	Li Yang is not here now.
Zhāng Lǎoshī míngtiān bú zài.	Prof. Zhang will not be in tomorrow.

Pattern Practice 2

Practice saying the following phrases.
Subject + **xìng** + surname

Wǒ xìng Wáng.	My last name is Wang.
Nèiwèi xiānsheng xìng Lín.	That gentleman's last name is Lin.
Wǒde jīnglǐ xìng Wú.	My manager's last name is Wu.
Wǒde Zhōngwén lǎoshī xìng Chén.	My Chinese teacher's last name is Chen.

Pattern Practice 3

Practice saying the following phrases.
Subject 1 + **gěi** (to/for) + Subject 2 + verb phrase

Wǒ míngtiān gěi nǐ dǎ diànhuà.	I will call you tomorrow.
Nǐ chángcháng gěi shéi dǎ diànhuà?	Who do you often call?
Wǒde māma chángcháng gěi wǒ dǎ diànhuà.	My mother often calls me.
Wǒ qǐng jīnglǐ gěi nín huí diàn.	I will ask the manager to call you back.

Wǒ qǐng jīnglǐ gěi nín huí diàn.

RECEPTIONIST

Pattern Practice 4

Practice saying the following phrases.
Subject + **huì** + verb phrase

Wǒ huì gěi Lín Jīnglǐ dǎ diànhuà.	I will call Manager Lin.
Wǒ míngtiān huì qù dǎ lánqiú.	I will go play basketball tomorrow.
Tā jīntiān huì qù mǎi yīfu.	He/She will go buy clothes today.
Nǐ huì qù Zhōngguó ma?	Will you be going to China?

Pattern Practice 5

Practice saying the following phrases.
Sentence + **le** indicating change of state

Wǒ zhīdàole.	Now I know. (I didn't know before).
Wǒ yǒu Zhōngwén míngzile.	Now I have a Chinese name. (I didn't have one before.)
Wǒmen yǒu zhōnghàode yīfule.	Now we have medium-sized shirts/dresses. (We didn't have them before).
Xiànzài bādiǎnle.	It's now 8 o'clock. (It was not 8 o'clock before this.)
Lǐ Yáng qù shítáng chīfànle.	Li Yang is going to the dining hall to eat. (He was doing something else before going to the dining hall to eat.)

EXERCISE 1

Fill in each blank with one of the following expressions.

gěi	xìng	wèi	wéi

1. **Nǐ jīntiān jǐdiǎn _____ wǒ dǎ diànhuà?**

2. A: **Qǐng wèn, nèi _____ shì...?**
   B: **Tā shì wǒde Měiguó péngyǒu.**

3. A: **_____, qǐng wèn, Lín Jīnglǐ zài ma?**
   B: **Tā zài. Qǐng děng** (wait) **yíxià.**

4. **Wǒ _____ Wáng, wǒ jiào Wáng Mǐn.**

EXERCISE 2

Answer each of the following questions in Chinese.

1. **Nǐ chángcháng gěi shéi dǎ diànhuà?**
2. **Nǐde shǒujī hàomǎ shì ...?**
3. **Nǐ sùshède diànhuà hàomǎ shì...?**

EXERCISE 3

Translate the following dialogues into Chinese.

1. A: Hello. Can I speak with Mr. Lin?
   B: He is not here right now. May I know who is calling?
   A: My last name is Li. I am a professor from the English Department.

2. A: I will ask Mr. Lin to call you back. What is your telephone number?
   B: My cell phone number is 138-8877-2266.
   A: Okay, I got it.

3. A: I have a Chinese name now.
   B: What is your Chinese name?
   A: My Chinese name is Dèng Róng.

EXERCISE 4

Task: Fill in the following registration form in Pinyin.

Registration Form
中文姓名: (Chinese Name)
国别: (Nationality)
职业别: (Occupation)
手机号码: (Cell phone number)
For Offical use only:

LESSON 12
Holiday Celebrations

Eric Goodman is chatting with Li Yang about Chinese holidays at the students'
cafeteria.

Eric:	Hey, Li Yang, what are the most important holidays in China?
	Èh, Lǐ Yáng, Zhōngguó zuì zhòngyàode jiérì shì shénme?
	唉，李洋，中国最重要的节日是什么？
Yang:	I think they are the Dragon Boat Festival, Mid-Autumn Festival, and the Chinese New Year.
	Wǒ juéde shì Duānwǔjié, Zhōngqiūjié hé nónglì Xīnnián ba!
	我觉得是端午节、中秋节和农历新年吧！
Eric:	When are these holidays?
	Zhèixiē jiérì shì shénme shíhou?
	这些节日是什么时候？
Yang:	The Dragon Boat Festival is on the fifth day of the fifth month, the Mid-Autumn Festival is on the fifteenth day of the eighth month, and the Chinese New Year is on the first day of the first month of the year.[1]
	Duānwǔjié shì Nónglì wǔyuè wǔhào, Zhōngqiūjié shì bāyuè shíwǔhào, nónglì Xīnnián shì yīyuè yīhào.
	端午节是农历五月五号，中秋节是八月十五号，农历新年是一月一号。
Eric:	How do Chinese people celebrate these holidays?
	Zhōngguó rén zěnme qìngzhù?
	中国人怎么庆祝？
Yang:	We eat glutinous rice dumplings during the Dragon Boat Festival, we eat mooncakes during the Mid-Autumn Festival, and we eat together with our families on Chinese New Year.
	Duānwǔjié wǒmen chī zòngzi, Zhōngqiūjié wǒmen chī yuèbǐng, nónglì Xīnnián wǒmen hé jiārén yìqǐ chīfàn.
	端午节我们吃粽子，中秋节我们吃月饼，农历新年我们和家人一起吃饭。
Eric:	Do Chinese people like Christmas too?
	Zhōngguó rén yě xǐhuan Shèngdànjié ma?
	中国人也喜欢圣诞节吗？

---

1   These dates are according to the Chinese lunar calendar.

Yang:	We like it more and more. We like to eat together with friends on Christmas.
	Yuèláiyuè xǐhuan, Shèngdànjié wǒmen xǐhuan hé péngyǒu chīfàn.
	越来越喜欢，圣诞节我们喜欢和朋友吃饭。

New Vocabulary

Pinyin	Chinese Character	English
Zuì	最	Most
Zhòngyào	重要	Important
Jiérì	节日	Holiday, festival
Duānwǔjié	端午节	Dragon Boat Festival
Zhōngqiūjié	中秋节	Mid-Autumn Festival
Hé	和	And, with
Nónglì	农历	Lunar calendar
Xīnnián	新年	New Year
Ba	吧	(Indicates assumption)
-Xiē	些	Some, a few
Zhèixiē	这些	These (at)
Shíhou	时候	Time, moment
Shénme shíhou	什么时候	When, what time
Wǔ	五	Five
Yuè	月	Month of the year
Hào	号	Day of the month
Shíwǔ	十五	Fifteen
Zěnme	怎么	How to
Qìngzhù	庆祝	Celebrate
Zòngzi	粽子	Glutinous rice dumplings
Yuèbǐng	月饼	Mooncake
Jiārén	家人	Family member(s)
Shèngdànjié	圣诞节	Christmas
Yuèláiyuè...	越来越	More and

Supplementary Vocabulary More Numbers

Pinyin	English
Shíyī	Eleven
Shí'èr	Twelve
Shísān	Thirteen
Shísì	Fourteen
Shíwǔ	Fifteen
Shíliù	Sixteen
Shíqī	Seventeen

Shíbā	Eighteen
Shíjiǔ	Nineteen
Èrshí	Twenty
Sānshí	Thirty
Sìshí	Forty
Wǔshí	Fifty
Liùshí	Sixty
Qīshí	Seventy
Bāshí	Eighty
Jiǔshí	Ninety

Supplementary Vocabulary Months of the Year[2]

Pinyin	English
Yīyuè	January
Èryuè	February
Sānyuè	March
Sìyuè	April
Wǔyuè	May
Liùyuè	June
Qīyuè	July
Bāyuè	August
Jiǔyuè	September
Shíyuè	October
Shíyīyuè	November
Shí'èryuè	December

Chinese Terms for Birthday and Western Holidays

Pinyin	English
shēngrì	Birthday
Wànshèngjié	Halloween; the Chinese version falls on the 15th day of the 7th month of the Lunar calendar
Gǎn'ēnjié	Thanksgiving
Qíngrénjié	Valentine's Day; the Chinese version falls on the 7th day of the 7th month of the Lunar calendar

---

2 **Yīyuè** (and all the other months) could refer to both the first month of the lunar year, as well as January depending on its context.

GRAMMAR NOTE The Superlative Marker **Zuì** = "Most"

Express superlatives with **zuì**, or "most". It can be followed by either a stative verb or a verb phrase. Examples:

zuì làde cài	the most spicy dish
zuì zhòngyàode jiérì	the most important holiday
Wǒ zuì xǐhuan chī Zhōngguó cài.	I like to eat Chinese food most.
Lǐ Yáng jīntiān zuì xiǎng chī zòngzi.	Li Yang wants to eat glutinous rice dumplings most today.

GRAMMAR NOTE Using the Word **Hé** = "And" or "With" as Conjunction or Coverb

There are two important usages with the word **hé**. First, **hé** is a conjunction word that connects two nouns. Examples:

wǒ hé nǐ	you and I
zòngzi hé yuèbǐng	glutinous rice dumplings and mooncakes
Zhōngguó hé Měiguó	China and the U.S.A.

If there are more than two nouns, **hé** needs to be inserted between the last two nouns, such as **Rìběn, Zhōngguó hé Měiguó** (Japan, China and the U.S.A.).

Helpful Tip:

Hé cannot be used to connect two sentences or verb phrases as the English word "and" can.

The other usage of **hé** is a coverb in the pattern "Subject 1 + **hé** + Subject 2 + verb phrase." Examples:

Nǐ xǐhuan hé shéi yìqǐ chīfàn?	Whom do you like to dine with?
Wǒ xǐhuan hé péngyǒu yìqǐ dǎ lánqiú.	I like to play basketball with friends.
Gāo Zhì'ān míngtiān huì hé Wáng Mǐn yìqǐ qù mǎi dōngxi.	Gao Zhi'an will be going to buy things together with Wang Min tomorrow.

In both usages, **hé** is equivalent to **gēn** despite regional preferences. In general, northerners use **hé** more while the southerners tend to use **gēn**. You will hear people say **hàn** in Taiwan.

GRAMMAR NOTE Using the Sentence Final Particle **Ba** = "I Suppose" to indicate Assumption or Supposition

Ba is a sentence final particle that implies the speaker's assumption or supposition. Compare:

Nǐ shì xuésheng.	You are a student. (statement)
Nǐ shì xuésheng ma?	Are you a student? (question)
Nǐ shì xuésheng ba?	You are a student, I suppose?

More examples with **ba**:

Gāo Zhì'ān shì Měiguó rén ba?	Gao Zhi'an is American, I suppose?
Zhōngqiūjié shì nónglì bāyuè ba?	The Mid-autumn Festival is in the lunar eighth month, I suppose?
Zhōngguó rén yě xǐhuan Shèngdànjié ba?	Chinese people also like Christmas, I suppose?

GRAMMAR NOTE Using The Word **Xiē** = "Some; a Few"

The word **xiē** is a measure word meaning "some". It needs to be preceded by a specifier (i.e., **zhèi**, **nèi**, or **něi**) and followed by a noun. Examples:

zhèixiē jiérì	these holidays
nèixiē rén	those people
něixiē yīfu	which pieces of clothes

GRAMMAR NOTE Using The Question Words **Shénme Shíhou** = "When"

In Lesson 6, you learned **jǐdiǎn** "what (clock) time." In this dialogue, you learn the question word **shénme shíhou** meaning "when." Examples:

Nǐ shénme shíhou qù Zhōngguó?	When are you going to China?
Zhōngguó rén shénme shíhou chī yuèbǐng?	When do Chinese people eat mooncakes?
Míngniánde nónglì Xīnnián shì shénme shíhou?	When is the Chinese New Year next year?

GRAMMAR NOTE **Using Yuè = "Month" and Hào = "Day of a Month" to Indicate Dates in a Month**

The word for "month" in Chinese is **yuè**. The twelve months of a year are included in the supplementary vocabulary. The word for "day of a month" is **hào**. To follow the principle of a big unit before a small unit mentioned in Lesson 6, the month always precedes the day. To ask "what day (of the month) is today," you can say **Jīntiān shì jǐyuè jǐhào?** More examples:

Duānwǔjié shì nónglì wǔyuè wǔhào.	The Dragon Boat Festival is on the fifth day of the fifth month.
Shèngdànjié shì shí'èryuè èrshíwǔhào.	Christmas is on December 25.
Wǒde shēngrì shì bāyuè bāhào.	My birthday is August 8.

GRAMMAR NOTE **Using Zěnme = "How" to ask how to do Something**

You have learned **zěnmeyàng** in the previous lessons meaning "How about" or "how someone is doing." In this lesson, you learn **zěnme** + verb to mean "how to verb." Examples:

Zěnme qìngzhù?	How to celebrate?
Zòngzi zěnme chī?	How do you eat glutinous rice dumplings?
Zài Zhōngguó zěnme dǎ diànhuà?	How do you make a phone call in China?

GRAMMAR NOTE **The Phrase Yuèláiyuè ... = "Increasingly"**

The pattern "**yuèláiyuè...**" can followed either by a stative verb or by a verb phrase. Examples:

Wǒde Zhōngwén yuèláiyuè hǎo.	My Chinese is improving.
Shèngdànjié zài Zhōngguó yuèláiyuè zhòngyào.	Christmas is becoming more important in China.
Zhōngguó rén yuèláiyuè xǐhuan Shèngdànjié.	Chinese people like Christmas more and more.
Gāo Zhì'ān yuèláiyuè xǐhuan Zhōngguó lìshǐ.	Gao Zhi'an likes Chinese history more and more.

CULTURAL NOTE — Chinese Traditional Holidays

Duānwǔjié, **Zhōngqiūjié** and **Nónglì Xīnnián** are considered the three most important holidays in Chinese culture. Each of these **jiérì** has its cultural rituals, festive food, and related folklore. For instance, the dragon boat tournament is held on **Duānwǔjié**, the story of Moon Goddess of Immortality **Cháng'é** is associated with **Zhōngqiūjié**, and the New Year's beast **Niánshòu** is associated with **Nónglì Xīnnián**.

CULTURAL NOTE — Chinese Lunar Calendar

Different from the Western calendar, the Chinese lunar calendar **nónglì** is an independent system of arranging dates, time, and seasons of the year largely based on the movement of the sun and the moon. Although nowadays the Western calendar has been officially adopted in Chinese societies, Chinese people frequently resort to **nónglì** when it comes to celebrating traditional holidays or selecting a day for weddings, funerals, or business grand openings.

CULTURAL NOTE — Zòngzi = "Glutinous Rice Dumplings" and Yuèbǐng = "Mooncakes"

Zòngzi is a pyramid-shaped traditional food made of glutinous rice. It contains various fillings such as pork, eggs, mushrooms, and is wrapped in bamboo leaves. **Zòngzi** is traditionally eaten on **Duānwǔjié**.

Yuèbǐng is a Chinese pastry with fillings such as red beans or pineapple paste with nuts. **Yuèbǐng** is traditionally consumed on **Zhōngqiūjié** and it fits perfectly with Chinese tea.

Pattern Practice 1

Practice saying the following phrases.
zuì + stative verb

zuì làde cài	the most spicy dish
zuì zhòngyàode jiérì	the most important holiday
zuì héshìde yīfu	the shirt/dress that fits best
zuì hǎode xuésheng	the best student

Pattern Practice 2

Practice saying the following phrases.
zuì + verb phrase

Wǒ zuì xǐhuan chī Zhōngguó cài.	I like to eat Chinese food most.
Wǒ zuì xǐhuan chī zòngzi.	I like to eat glutinous rice dumplings the most.
Nǐ zuì xiǎng qù nǎr?	Where do you want to go most?
Gāo Zhì'ān zuì xiǎng xué Zhōngguó lìshǐ.	Gao Zhi'an wants to study Chinese history most.

Pattern Practice 3

Practice saying the following phrases.
Noun 1 + hé + Noun 2

Měiguó zuì zhòngyàode jiérì shì Gǎn'ēnjié hé Shèngdànjié.	The most important holidays in the US are Thanksgiving and Christmas.
Wǒ xiǎng xué Zhōngwén hé Rìwén.	I want to study the Chinese and Japanese languages.
Wǒ mǎi zhèijiàn yīfu hé nèijiàn kùzi.	I am buying this shirt/dress and that pair of pants.
Zhāng Lǎoshī míngtiān qù Měiguó hé Jiānádà.	Professor Zhang is going to the US and Canada tomorrow.

Pattern Practice 4

Practice saying the following phrases.
Subject 1 + hé + Subject 2 + verb phrase

Wǒ chángcháng hé péngyǒu chīfàn.	I often eat with friends.
Nǐ chángcháng hé jiārén chīfàn ma?	Do you often eat with your family?
Lǐ Yáng míngtiān hé Gāo Zhì'ān yìqǐ dǎ lánqiú.	Li Yang will play basketball with Gao Zhi'an tomorrow.
Wáng Mǐn jīntiān wǎnshàng hé péngyǒu qù mǎi dōngxi.	Wang Min is going to buy things with her friends tonight.

Pattern Practice 5

Practice saying the following phrases.
Statement + ba indicating assumption or supposition

Míngtiān shì xīngqītiān ba?	Tomorrow is Sunday, I suppose?
Nǐ shì xuésheng ba?	You are a student, I suppose?
Nǐ zuìjìn hěn máng ba?	You have been busy recently, I suppose?
"Gāo Zhì'ān" shì nǐde Zhōngwén míngzi ba?	Gao Zhi'an is your Chinese name, I suppose?

Pattern Practice 6

Practice saying the following phrases.
Event/Holiday + **shì** + **shénme shíhou**

Duānwǔjié shì shénme shíhou?   When is the Dragon Boat Festival?
Zhōngqiūjié shì shénme shíhou?   When is the Mid-autumn Festival?
Gǎn'ēnjié shì shénme shíhou?   When is Thanksgiving?
Zhōngguóde Qíngrénjié shì shénme   When is the Chinese Valentine's Day?
  shíhou?

Pattern Practice 7

Practice saying the following phrases.
Subject + **shénme shíhou** + verb phrase

Nǐ shénme shíhou gěi tā dǎ diànhuà?   When are you calling him/her?
Nǐ shénme shíhou qù chīfàn?   When are you going to eat?
Zhōngguó rén shénme shíhou chī   When do Chinese people eat
  yuèbǐng?   mooncakes?
Zhōngguó rén shénme shíhou   When do Chinese people eat glutinous
  chī zòngzi?   rice dumplings?

Pattern Practice 8

Practice saying the following phrases.
Yuèlái yuè + stative verb/verb phrase

Zuìjìn dōngxi yuèláiyuè guì.   Things are getting increasingly
                                            expensive recently.

Hǎode cānguǎn yuèláiyuè duō.   There are more and more good
                                            restaurants.

Tā zuìjìn yuèlái yuè máng.   He/She has been busier and busier
                                            recently.

Wǒ yuèláiyuè xǐhuan yùndòng.	I like exercising more and more.
Gāo Zhì'ān yuèláiyuè xǐhuan Zhōngguó lìshǐ.	Gao Zhi'an likes Chinese history more and more.

Pattern Practice 9

Zhèi/Nèi/Něi + xiē + noun

Zhèixiē jiérì zhòngyào ma?	Are these holidays important?
Nèixiē rén zài ma?	Are those people around?
Něixiē yīfu nǐ bù xǐhuan?	Which of these clothes don't you like?

EXERCISE 1

Fill in each blank with one of the following expressions.

xiē	zěnme	zuì	hé

1. Nǐ chángcháng _____ shéi yìqǐ chīfàn?

2. Nèi _____ rén shì shéi?

3. Wǒ juéde Měiguó _____ zhòngyàode jiérì shì Shèngdànjié.

4. Zhōngguó rén _____ qìngzhù Nónglì Xīnnián?

EXERCISE 2

Answer each of the following questions in Chinese.

1. Nǐde guójiā (country) zuì zhòngyàode jiérì shì shénme?
2. Nǐde shēngrì shì jǐyuè jǐhào?
3. Nǐ zěnme qìngzhù Xīnnián?

EXERCISE 3

Translate the following dialogues into Chinese.

1. A: When is the Chinese New Year?
   B: It's on the first day of the first month.
   A: How do Chinese people celebrate this holiday?
   B: They eat together with their families.

2. A: When do Chinese people eat mooncakes?
   B: We eat mooncakes during the Mid-autumn Festival. Do you like mooncakes?
   A: I'm liking them more and more.

3. A: What is the most important holiday in China?
   B: I think it's Chinese New Year. What about the US?
   A: I think it's Christmas.

EXERCISE 4

Task: Below are the six important holidays in China. You have been introduced three of them in this lesson. Check out the other three holidays online and write down their names in English.

Jǐyuè Jǐhào (Date)	Shénme Jiérì (? Holidays)
Nónglì yīyuè yīhào	
Sìyuè wǔhào	
Wǔyuè yīhào	
Nónglì wǔyuè wǔhào	
Nónglì bāyuè shíwǔhào	
Shíyuè yīhào	

LESSON 13
Feeling Unwell

:::: DIALOGUE :::: Expressing Concern

Wang Min bumps into Eric Goodman on campus. She notices that Eric looks a bit pale and seems to be sick.

Min: Gao Zhi'an, what happened? You look a little bit sick.
                Gāo Zhì'ān, zěnmele? Nǐ kànqilai yǒuyìdiǎnr bù shūfu.
                高志安，怎么了？你看起来有一点儿不舒服。

Eric: I caught a cold.
                Wǒ gǎnmàole.
                我感冒了。

Min: Did you go see a doctor?
                Qù kànle yīshēng ma?
                去看了医生吗？

Eric: I did yesterday.
                Zuótiān kànle.
                昨天看了。

Min: What did the doctor say?
                Yīshēng shuō shénme?
                医生说什么？

Eric: The doctor said I caught a cold. He prescribed some medicine for me and asked me to get more rest.
                Yīshēng shuō wǒ gǎnmàole, gěi wǒ kāile yìxiē yào, yào wǒ duō xiūxi.
                医生说我感冒了，给我开了一些药，要我多休息。

Min: Have more rest then. Also, drink more water!
                Nà nǐ duō xiūxi ba, yě duō hē shuǐ.
                那你多休息吧，也多喝水。

Eric: Okay, thank you.
                Hǎo, xièxie.
                好，谢谢。

New Vocabulary

Pinyin	Chinese Character	English
Zěnmele	怎么了	"What's wrong", "what happened"
Kàn	看	See, look
Kànqilai	看起来	Seem, look like
Yǒuyìdiǎn(r)	一点儿	A little
Shūfu	舒服	Comfortable, physically well
Gǎnmào	感冒	Catch a cold

New Vocabulary (cont'd)

Pinyin	Chinese Character	English
-Le	了	(Indicates completion of the action)
Yīshēng	医生	Medical doctor, title as term of address
Zuótiān	昨天	Yesterday
Shuō	说	Say, speak
Kāiyào	开药	Prescribe medicine
Yìxiē	一些	Some, a few
Duō	多	More
Xiūxi	休息	Rest (v)
Ba	吧	(Indicates suggestions)
Hē	喝	Drink (v)
Shuǐ	水	Water (v)

Supplementary Vocabulary   Common Symptoms When Having a Cold

Pinyin	English
Fāshāo	Have a fever
Méiyou lìqi	Have no strength
Tóuténg	Have a headache

Other Common Verb Phrases That Go With Duō/Shǎo

Pinyin	English
Duō hē chá	Drink more tea
Duō shuìjiào	Sleep more
Duō yùndòng	Exercise more
Duō liànxí shuō Zhōngwén	Practice speaking Chinese more
Shǎo hē kāfēi	Have less coffee
Shǎo mǎi dōngxi	Buy fewer things

GRAMMAR NOTE

Using the Word Shūfu = "Comfortable, Physically Well" to Describe Physical Conditions

Shūfu is a stative verb meaning "comfortable" or "physically well." Examples:

Jīntiān hěn shūfu.	(The weather) is comfortable today.
Wǒ jīntiān yǒuyìdiǎnr bù shūfu.	I am not feeling well today.

GRAMMAR NOTE

Using the Adverb yuyìdiǎnr = "A Little Bit ..." to Describe Something Negative

When talking about something negative or unpleasant, such as bù shūfu (sick) or hěn yóu (greasy) Chinese people who are not close with each other tend to avoid direct comments by adding yǒuyìdiǎnr in front of the stative verb. Examples:

Wǒ jīntiān yǒuyìdiǎnr bù shūfu.	I am a bit uncomfortable today.

Zhèige cài yǒuyìdiǎnr yóu.	This dish is a bit greasy.
Nèijiàn yīfu yǒuyìdiǎnr guì.	That shirt/dress is a bit expensive.

Therefore, if Eric Goodman emails Professor Zhang informing him of his absence because he's sick, instead of saying **Wǒ jīntiān hěn bù shūfu**, he should say **Wǒ jīntiān yǒuyìdiǎnr bù shūfu**. Similarly, if Professor Zhang asks Eric, **Nǐ zuìjìn zěnmeyàng**, instead of saying **Wǒ hěn máng**, he should say **Wǒ yǒuyìdiǎnr máng**.

Helpful Tip:
Do not confuse **yǒuyìdiǎnr** + negative stative verb with **Wǒ yǒuyìdiǎnr shìr** you learned in Lesson 6. The structure of **Wǒ yǒu yìdiǎnr shìr** is "Subject + **yǒu** + **yìdiǎnr** + noun".

GRAMMAR NOTE Using the Resultative Compound Verb Kànqǐlai = "Seem; Look Like"

This verb-resultative compound **kànqǐlai** is composed of the verb **kàn** "to see, look" and the resultative compound **qǐlai** "the performing of the action." **Kànqǐlai** usually appears in the "Subject + **kànqǐlai** + **hěn/bù** + stative verb" pattern. Examples:

Nǐ jīntiān kànqǐlai hěn lèi.	You look tired today.
Zhèige cài kànqǐlai hěn hǎochī.	This dish looks delicious.
Zhèijiàn tīxùshān kànqǐlai yǒuyìdiǎnr xiǎo.	This t-shirt looks a bit small.

GRAMMAR NOTE Using the Verb Gǎnmào = "Catch a Cold"

Gǎnmào, meaning "cold", like many other symptoms listed in the Supplementary Vocabulary, functions as verb in Chinese. **Le** here is mandatory to indicate the completion of the verb **gǎnmào**. It is ungrammatical to say **Wǒ gǎnmào** or **Wǒ yǒu gǎnmào**. Examples:

Wǒ gǎnmàole.	I have a cold.
Gāo Zhì'ān hé tāde péngyǒu dōu gǎnmàole.	Gao Zhi'an and his friends all have colds.

GRAMMAR NOTE "Verb + le" Indicates Completion of an Action

You have learned Sentence + **le** in Lesson 11 to indicate a change of state. In this lesson, **le** is placed after a verb to mean that the action of the verb is completed. Compare the following statements:

Wǒ kàn yīshēng.	I'm going to visit the doctor.
Wǒ kànle yīshēng.	I've seen (visited) the doctor already.

Nǐ chī yuèbǐng ma?	Do you eat mooncakes?
Nǐ chīle yuèbǐng ma?	Have you eaten the mooncakes already?

Nǐ gěi Lín Jīnglǐ dǎ diànhuà ma?	Are you calling Manager Lin?
Nǐ gěi Lín Jīnglǐ dǎle diànhuà ma?	Have you called Manager Lin?

GRAMMAR NOTE
Using the Word **kāiyào** = "Prescribe Medicine"

As a verb **kāi** + object **yào** compound, other components such as **le** or attributives (e.g. **yìxiē** "some") can be inserted between **kāi** and **yào**. Examples:

Yīshēng kāile yào.	The doctor prescribed medicine.
Yīshēng kāile yìxiē yào.	The doctor prescribed some medicine.

To say "take medicine," use **chīyào** (literally, eat medicine).

GRAMMAR NOTE
Using the Pattern **Duō/Shǎo** + Verb Phrase = "Verb Phrase More/Less" to give Advice

If you want to advise someone to do something more or less, the pattern in Chinese is **duō/shǎo** + verb phrase. (Other common verb phrases can be found in the supplementary vocabulary.) Examples:

Duō xiūxi.	Rest more.
Duō hē shuǐ.	Drink more water.
Shǎo hē kāfēi.	Have less coffee.

GRAMMAR NOTE
The Sentence Final Particle **Ba** = Suggestions

You have learned the sentence final **ba** indicating supposition in Lesson 12. Examples:

Gāo Zhì'ān shì Měiguó rén ba?	Gao Zhi'an is American, I suppose?
Zhōngqiūjié shì nónglì bāyuè ba?	The Mid-autumn Festival is in August, I suppose?

In this lesson, you learn the other useful usage of the sentence final **ba** to indicate a suggestion and soften the statement. The affirmative response to this suggestion with **ba** is usually **hǎo** meaning agreement "okay." Compare:

Qù kàn yīshēng.	Go see a doctor. (command)
Qù kàn yīshēng ba.	I suggest you go see a doctor. (suggestion)

Duō shuìjiào.	Get more sleep. (command)
Duō shuìjiào ba.	I suggest you get more sleep. (suggestion)
Nǐ mǎi zhōnghàode.	You buy the middle size one. (command)
Nǐ mǎi zhōnghàode ba.	I suggest you buy the middle sized one. (suggestion)

GRAMMAR NOTE   Connecting Two Verb Phrases or Sentences

As mentioned in Lesson 8, the Chinese language does not require a conjunction word to connect two verb phrases such as **duō xiūxi** and **duō hē shuǐ**. Remember, it is ungrammatical to say **Nǐ duō xiūxi hé duō hē shuǐ**. However, you can add the adverb **yě** in front of the second verb phrase to mean "also."

CULTURAL NOTE   **Zěnmele** to Show your Concern

Zěnmele means "What happened?" or "What's wrong?" It is used to show the speaker's care or concern about the listener. You can ask "**Nǐ zěnmele?**" if you see your friend in a bad mood. Do not confuse **zěnmele** with **zěnmeyàng**. **Zěnmele** is to show your care or concerns while **zěnmeyàng** is to ask how someone is doing or inquire about opinions.

Pattern Practice 1

Practice saying the following phrases.
Subject + **yǒuyìdiǎnr** + negative stative verb

Wǒ jīntiān yǒuyìdiǎnr bù shūfu.	I feel a bit sick today.
Wǒ zuìjìn yǒuyìdiǎnr máng.	I have been a bit busy recently.
Zhèige cānguǎnde cài yǒuyìdiǎnr yóu.	The food in this restaurant is a bit greasy.
Nèijiàn chènyī yǒuyìdiǎnr guì.	That shirt is a bit expensive.
Zhōngwén yǒuyìdiǎnr nán.	Chinese is a bit difficult.

Pattern Practice 2

Practice saying the following phrases.
Subject + **kànqǐlai** + **hěn** or **bù** + stative verb

Lǐ Yáng jīntiān kànqǐlai hěn lèi.	Li Yang looks tired today.
Zòngzi kànqǐlai hěn hǎochī.	Glutinous dumplings look tasty.
Zhèijiàn tīxùshān kànqǐlai hěn héshì.	This t-shirt fits well.
Nèige shítáng kànqǐlai bú dà.	That dining hall doesn't look big.

Pattern Practice 3

Practice saying the following phrases.
Subject + verb + **le** + (noun)

Wǒ gǎnmàole.	I have a cold.
Wǒ chīle.	I ate.
Wǒ zuótiān qù kànle yīshēng.	I went to see a doctor yesterday.
Wáng Mǐn jīntiān qùle túshūguǎn.	Wang Min went to the library today.
Zuótiān shì Zhōngqiūjié. Nǐ chīle yuèbǐng ma?	It was the Mid-autumn Festival yesterday. Did you eat mooncakes?

Pattern Practice 4

Practice saying the following phrases.
Duō/Shǎo + verb phrase

Duō xiūxi.	Rest more.
Duō hē shuǐ.	Drink more water.
Duō yùndòng.	Exercise more.
Shǎo hē kāfēi.	Have less coffee.
Shǎo chī làde cài.	Eat spicy food less.
Shǎo chī yóude cài.	Eat greasy food less.

Pattern Practice 5

Practice saying the following phrases.
Statement + **ba** indicating suggestion

Duō shuìjiào ba.	I suggest you get more sleep.
Duō xiūxi ba.	I suggest you have more rest.
Nǐ mǎi dàhàode ba.	I suggest you buy the large size.
Wǒmen qù Zhōngguó ba.	I suggest we go to China.
Nǐ gěi Lín Jīnglǐ huí diàn ba.	I suggest you return Manager Lin's phone call.

EXERCISE 1

Fill in each blank with one of the following expressions.

ba	shǎo	kāi	duō	gǎnmào

1. Wǒ _____ le, yǒuyìdiǎnr bù shūfu.

2. Yīshēng gěi wǒ _____ le yìxiē yào.

3. Nǐ _____ yùndòng, _____ shàngwǎng.

4. A: Wǒmen qù chīfàn _____!
   B: Hǎo. Wǒmen qù nǎr chī?

EXERCISE 2

Translate the following dialogues into Chinese.

1. A: Hey, what's wrong? You don't look well today.
   B: I caught a cold.
   A: Did you go see a doctor?
   B: Yes, I went with my friend yesterday.

2. A: What did the doctor say?
   B: He said that I needed to take more rest and drink more water.
   A: Did he prescribe any medicine?
   B: Yes, he prescribed me some medicine.

3. A: Did you take your medicine today?
   B: I did.
   A: Have more rest then.
   B: I will, thank you.

EXERCISE 3

Role Playing

You bump into your Chinese friend today on campus. You notice that your Chinese friend doesn't look physically well. Show your concerns by asking (1) what happened, and (2) if he/she went to see a doctor. End your conversation by giving him/her some advice to feel better.

LESSON 14
Being Invited to the Manager's Home for Dinner (I)

DIALOGUE Arriving at The Manager's Home

After having known Eric Goodman for a few months, Manager Lin invites Eric to his home for dinner. Eric arrives and brings a little gift for Manager Lin.

Manager:	Gao Zhi'an, you are here.
	Gāo Zhì'ān, nǐ lái le.
	高志安，你来了。
Eric:	Hi, Manager.
	Jīnglǐ, nín hǎo.
	经理，您好。
Manager:	Please come in.
	Lái, qǐng jìn.
	来，请进。
Eric:	Thank you. Should I take off my shoes?
	Xièxie, yào tuō xié ma?
	谢谢，要脱鞋吗？
Manager:	Yes, here are the slippers.
	En, zhèr yǒu tuōxié.
	嗯，这儿有拖鞋。
Eric:	Manager, this is a small token of appreciation (for you).
	Jīnglǐ, zhè shì yīdiǎnr xiǎoyìsi.
	经理，这是一点儿小意思。
Manager:	Oh, you are too polite. Please do not bring a gift next time.
	Āi, nǐ tài kèqile, xiàcì bié dài dōngxi.
	哎，你太客气了，下次别带东西。
Eric:	It's nothing, just something I should do.
	Nàli, yīnggāide.
	哪里，应该的。

New Vocabulary

Pinyin	Chinese Character	English
Lái	来	Come (indicates invitation)
Jìn	进	Enter *(v)*
Yào	要	Need to, should
Tuō	脱	Take off
Xié	鞋	Shoe(s)
Zhèr	这儿	Here

New Vocabulary (cont'd)

Pinyin	Chinese Character	English
Tuōxié	拖鞋	Slippers, sandals
Xiǎoyìsi	小意思	Little gift, small token of appreciation
Kèqi	客气	Polite
Xiàcì	下次	Next time
-Cì	次	Time
Bié	别	Don't
Dài	带	Bring
Yīnggāide	应该的	"Something I ought to do"

GRAMMAR NOTE ## Using **Lái** = "Come" to Indicate Motion Toward the Speaker or a Gesture of Invitation

Lái means "come" and it indicates motion toward the speaker. Examples:

Nǐ shénme shíhou lái Běijīng?	When are you coming to Beijing? (The speaker is in Beijing.)
Wǒ lái Qīnghuá Dàxué yùndòng.	I come to Tsinghua University to exercise. (The speaker is at Tsinghua University.)
Wǒ lái Zhōngguó xué Zhōngwén.	I have come to China to study the Chinese language. (The speaker is in China.)

Lái can also be used in the beginning of an utterance indicating a gesture of invitation. The meaning of the utterance remains the same without **lái**. Examples:

Lái, qǐng jìn.	Please come in.
Lái, qǐng zuò.	Please have a seat.
Lái, wǒmen chīfàn ba.	Let's eat.

GRAMMAR NOTE ## Using the Word **Yào** = "Should" or "Need to"

You have learned **yào** meaning "want" in the previous lesson. In this lesson, **yào** means "should" or "need to" and it needs to be placed between the subject and the verb phrase. Examples:

Wǒ yào tuō xié ma?	Do I need to take off my shoes?
Nǐ gǎnmàole, yào duō xiūxi.	You caught a cold. You need to get more rest.
Mǎi yīfu nǐ yào shìchuān.	You need to try them on when you buy clothes.

To negate, use **bú yòng** instead of **bú yào**:

Nǐ bú yòng tuō xié.	You don't need to take off (your) shoes.
Wǒ bú yòng shìchuān.	I don't need to try them on.
Nǐ bú yòng gěi wǒ dǎ diànhuà.	You don't need to call me.

GRAMMAR NOTE   Using the Pattern Place + **Yǒu** + Noun = "There is/are Noun(s) in Place"

In Lesson 7, you learned that place words in Chinese often serve as the subjects in a sentence. In this lesson, a place word is followed by **yǒu** + noun to mean "There is/are noun(s) in place." Examples:

Zhèr yǒu tuōxié.	There are slippers here.
Zhèr yǒu yìxiē yào.	There is some medicine here.
Zhōngguó yǒu sānge zhòngyàode jiérì.	There are three important holidays in China.

GRAMMAR NOTE   Using the Measure Word **Cì** = "Time"

Cì is a measure word meaning "time." The three most common compounds with **cì** are:

zhèicì	this time	**shàngcì**	last time	**xiàcì**	next time

These three compounds function as time words, so they can be put either in the beginning of a sentence or between the subject and the verb phrase. Examples:

Nǐ zhèicì yào mǎi shénme?	What do you want to buy this time?
Nǐ shàngcì qùle nǎr?	Where did you go last time?
Xiàcì nǐ bié dài dōngxi.	(You) Don't bring things next time.

CULTURAL NOTE   The Greeting **Nǐ Lái Le** = "You Have Come"

Nǐ lái le is a common greeting when a host sees the guest has arrived. The sentence final **le** indicates the change of state of the guest's arrival.

CULTURAL NOTE   Being a House Guest in Chinese Culture

Visiting other people's house as a guest involves various customs and formulaic expressions in every culture, and China is no exception. In this lesson, you will learn the following aspects:

(1) Shoes

When you enter a Chinese house, it is customary to remove your shoes and put on the **tuōxié** (slippers) the host prepares for you. Do not confuse the verb phrase **tuō xié** (take off shoes) with the noun **tuōxié** (sandals, slippers). They are homonyms, but the Chinese written characters are different.

(2) Gifts

When you visit a Chinese house, always bring a **xiǎoyìsi** (little gift) or **xiǎodōngxi** (little things), such as fruit, tea leaves, or pastries. The gift does not need to be extravagant, but it should be nicely packed or wrapped. The reason of bringing gifts is to show your appreciation of the host's invitation. **Xiǎoyìsi**, literally meaning "a small token of appreciation," is an idiomatic expression frequently used when someone presents a gift. **Xiǎo** here does not reflect the actual value of the gift; it is merely used for the purpose of remaining humble.

(3) The Concept of Kèqi = Politeness

Kèqi (politeness) is an important and well-appreciated social value in Chinese society. Its purpose is to maintain social and interpersonal harmony through interactions, behaviors, and the language. The expressions you have learned, such as **qǐng** + verb, **yǒuyìdiǎnr** + negative stative verb, and **bú tài**... are all examples of showing how **kèqi** you are. **Nǐ hěn kèqi** "You are very polite" in Chinese is always a compliment.

Kèqi is expected from both parties in a host-guest scenario and many formulaic expressions are involved. For instance, the manager accepts the gift by saying **Nǐ tài kèqile** "You're too kind/polite" instead of **xièxie**. When accepting a gift, Chinese people tend to comment first on the good intention of the gift-giver then on the gift. Also note that **Nǐ tài kèqile** is a response by a gift-receiver of higher status. If Eric Goodman receives a gift from the manager, **Nǐ tài kèqile** will not be appropriate. Instead, Eric could say **Zhè zěnme hǎoyìsi?** "How do I deserve your good intention?".

The other common idiomatic expression **yīnggāide** or "This is something I ought to do" is often used by the gift-giver when the host expresses that the gift is not necessary. Of course, the reason the host says that the gift is not necessary is because he/she is being **kèqi**, not because he/she does not appreciate the guest's good intention.

Pattern Practice 1

Practice saying the following phrases.
Subject + **yào** + verb phrase

Nǐ yào duō yùndòng.	You should exercise more.
Nǐ yào duō hē shuǐ.	You need to drink more water.
Nǐ yào duō xiūxi.	You should rest more.
Nǐ yào duō gěi jiārén dǎ diànhuà.	You should call your family more.
Nǐ yào shǎo chī lade cài.	You need to eat less spicy food.
Nǐ yào chī yào.	You need to take medicine.
Nǐ yào dài yìdiǎnr dōngxi.	You should bring a little gift.

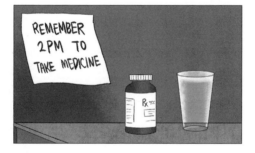

Pattern Practice 2

Practice saying the following phrases.
Subject + **bú yòng** + verb phrase

Nǐ bú yòng gěi wǒ dǎ diànhuà.	You don't need to call me.
Nǐ bú yòng chī yào.	You don't need to take any medicine.
Nǐ bú yòng dài dōngxi.	You don't need to bring things.
Nǐ bú yòng tōngzhī jīnglǐ.	You don't need to inform the manager.

Pattern Practice 3

Practice saying the following phrases.
Place + **yǒu** + noun

Běijīng Dàxué yǒu jǐge shítáng?	How many dining halls does Peking University have?
Běijīng Dàxué yǒu jǐge yùndòng zhōngxīn?	How many sports centers does Peking University have?
Zhèr yǒu diànhuà ma?	Is there a telephone here?
Zhèr yǒu cānguǎn ma?	Is there a restaurant here?
Zhōngguó yǒu sānge zhòngyàode jiérì.	There are three important holidays in China.

Pattern Practice 4

Practice saying the following phrases.
Subject + **zhèicì/shàngcì/xiàcì** + verb phrase

Nǐ zhèicì yào qù nǎr?	Where are you going this time?
Nǐ shàngcì chīle shénme?	What did you eat last time?
Nǐ xiàcì kéyi gěi wǒ dǎ diànhuà.	You can call me next time.
Wǒmen xiàcì yìqǐ chīfàn ba.	Let's eat together next time.
Nǐ zhèicì yào fùxiàn háishì shuākǎ?	Do you want to pay cash or with a credit card this time?

EXERCISE 1

Fill in each blank with one of the following expressions.

yào	yǒu	cì	lái

1. ————, qǐng zuò.

2. Qǐng wèn, nǎr ———— kāfēidiàn?

3. Nǐ ———— duō xiūxi. Nǐ tài mángle.

4. Nǐ tài kèqile, xià ———— bié dài dōngxi.

EXERCISE 2

Translate the following dialogues into Chinese.

1. A: Here you are. Please come in.
   B: Thank you.

2. A: Do I need to take off my shoes?
   B: Yes, here are the slippers.
   A: Thank you.

3. A: This is a small token of appreciation.
   B: You are too polite. Don't bring things next time.
   A: You are welcome. This is something I ought to do.

EXERCISE 3

Task: Below are the common gifts Chinese people bring when they visit others' houses. Practice presenting each gift to the host by following the dialogue below.

You: **Zhè shì yīdiǎnr...**
Host: **Nǐ tài kèqile**
You: **Nǎli, yīnggāide.**

Chinese	English
shuǐguǒ	fruit
cháyè	tea leaves
bǐng	biscuits, cookies, pastries
dàngāo	cakes

LESSON 15
Being Invited to the Manager's Home for Dinner (II)

DIALOGUE Asking about Family

Eric Goodman sees a family picture on the wall. Out of curiosity, he asks Manager Lin about his family.

Eric:	Manager, how many people are there in your family?
	Jīnglǐ, nín jiā yǒu jǐge rén?
	经理，您家有几个人？
Manager:	There are four—my wife, my two children, and me.
	Sìge, wǒ, wǒ tàitai, hé liǎngge háizi.
	四个，我、我太太和两个孩子。
Eric:	How old are your children this year?
	Háizi jīnnián jǐsuìle?
	孩子今年几岁了？
Manager:	My son is eight years old. My daughter is older than my son. She is ten years old.
	Érzi bāsuì, nǚ'ér bǐ érzi dà, jīnnián shísuì.
	儿子八岁，女儿比儿子大，今年十岁。
Eric:	(points to a picture on the wall) Is that your wife?
	Nèiwèi jiù shì nínde tàitai ma?
	那位就是您的太太吗？
Manager:	Yes. Come, have more food.
	Duì. Lái, duō chī diǎnr, duō chī diǎnr.
	对。来，多吃点儿，多吃点儿。
Eric:	Okay.
	Hǎo.
	好。
Manager:	Would you like to have some wine?
	Nǐ yào hē jiǔ ma?
	你要喝酒吗？
Eric:	No, thank you. I have to drive.
	Bú yòng, xièxie, wǒ děi kāichē.
	不用，谢谢，我得开车。

New Vocabulary

Pinyin	Chinese Character	English
Jiā	家	Family, home
Tàitai	太太	Wife
Liǎng	两	Two
Háizi	孩子	Child, kid
Nián	今	Year
Jīnnián	今年	This year
Suì	岁	Years of age
Jǐsuì	几岁	How many years old (for someone under ten)
Érzi	儿子	Son
Nǚ'ér	女儿	Daughter
Bǐ	比	Compare
Shí	十	Ten
Jiù	就	Exactly, precisely
Jiǔ	酒	Wine, alcohol
Bú yòng	不用	Don't need to
Děi	得	Must
Kāichē	开车	Drive (v)

Supplementary Vocabulary   Familial Relationships

Pinyin	English
Bàba	Father
Māma	Mother
Gēge	Older brother
Jiějie	Older sister
Dìdi	Younger brother
Mèimei	Younger sister

GRAMMAR NOTE   Omitting **De** in the "Pronoun + **De** + Noun" Pattern

When you refer to people close to you or to the person you are conversing with, such as jiā "family" or "family members", the possessive marker **de** is optional. Examples:

Wǒ(de) jiā	my family
Wǒ(de) tàitai	My wife
Nǐ(de) háizi	Your children

GRAMMAR NOTE Using the Term **Jiā** = "Family" or "Home"

The term **jiā** means "family" or "home," but not "house" as a building. Examples:

Nǐ jiā yǒu jǐge rén?	How many people are there in your family?
Nǐ jiā zài nǎr?	Where is your home?
Wǒde jiā zài Měiguó, bú zài Zhōngguó.	My home is in the US, not in China.

GRAMMAR NOTE Using **Liǎng** in Pairs and **Èr** as Numeral

Both **liǎng** and **èr** mean "two." However, they are completely different in usage. **Èr** is a digit or a number. **Liǎng** is closer to the idea of "a pair" and needs to be followed by a measure word. Examples:

Wǒde shǒujī hàomǎ shì 139-2227-6688.	My cellphone number is 139-2227-6688.
Jīntiān shì èryuè wǔhào.	Today is February 5th.
Wǒ yǒu liǎngge háizi.	I have two children.
Wǒ yǒu liǎngjiàn kùzi.	I have two pairs of pants.
Zhèi liǎngwèi lǎoshī shì Táiwān rén.	These two teachers are Taiwanese.

Helpful Tip:
The best way to differentiate **liǎng** from **èr** is to remember the difference between **èr yuè** (February) and **liǎngge yuè** (two months).

GRAMMAR NOTE The Word **Suì** = "Years old"

Do distinguish between the following three ways to ask about someone's age, even though in English they all mean "how old are you":

1. Younger than ten years old: **Nǐ jǐsuìle?**
2. Older than ten years old: **Nǐ duō dàle?**
3. People above 50 years old: **Nín duō dà niánjìle?**

The **le** in the three examples above indicates change of state and is optional. To respond, simply follow the pattern "Subject + number + **suì** + (**le**)". Examples:

Wǒ shíbāsuì.	I am eighteen years old.
Wǒ bàba liùshísuì.	My father is sixty years old.
Tāde tàitai jīnnián wǔshísuìle.	His wife is fifty years old this year.

GRAMMAR NOTE   Noun 1 + **Bǐ** + Noun 2 + Stative Verb = Comparison

To compare two nouns, we use the above sentence structure, to show that one is more of something than the other, e.g., harder, older or tastes better. Examples:

Lín Jīnglǐde nǚ'ér bǐ érzi dà.	Manager Lin's daughter is older than his son.
Wǒ juéde Zhōngwén bǐ Rìwén nán.	I feel that Chinese is harder than Japanese.
Cānguǎnde cài bǐ shítángde cài hǎochī.	The food in the restaurants tastes better than the dining hall's food.

The examples above can also be expressed by using **bǐjiào** (Lesson 9):

Lín Jīnglǐde nǚ'ér bǐjiào dà.	Manager Lin's daughter is older.
Wǒ juéde Zhōngwén bǐjiào nán.	I feel that Chinese is harder.
Cānguǎnde cài bǐjiào hǎochī.	The food in the restaurants tastes better.

Helpful Tips:
Do not add **hěn** in front of the stative verb in this "Noun 1 + **bǐ** + Noun 2 + stative verb" pattern. It is ungrammatical to say **Zhōngwén bǐ Rìwén hěn nán**, literally "Chinese harder than Japanese very difficult".

GRAMMAR NOTE   The Adverb **Jiù** = "Exactly, Precisely"

The adverb **jiù**, meaning "exactly, precisely," is used to emphasize information. It needs to be put between the subject and the verb phrase. Compare:

Zhèiwèi shì Lín Jīnglǐde tàitai.	This is Manager Lin's wife. (general statement)
Zhèiwèi jiù shì Lín Jīnglǐde tàitai.	This is Manager Lin's wife. (emphasize with **jiù**)
Zhè shì yuèbǐng.	This is a mooncake. (general statement)
Zhè jiù shì yuèbǐng.	This is a mooncake. (emphasize with **jiù**)

You can also use **jiù** when you answer a phone call and identify yourself. Suppose you are Manager Lin. When someone calls your office and says **Wéi, qǐng wèn, Lín Jīnglǐ zài ma** ("Hello, can I speak with Manager Lin?"), you can answer "**Wǒ jiù shì** (speaking)."

GRAMMAR NOTE   The Auxiliary Verb **Děi** = "Must, Necessity"

The auxiliary verb **děi** that indicates that the action is a necessity, or obligation, needs to be placed between the subject and the verb phrase. Examples:

Nǐ gǎnmàole, děi duō xiūxi.	You have a cold. You must rest more.
Nǐ zài Zhōngguórénde jiā děi tuō xié.	You must take off your shoes in a Chinese home.
Qù Zhōngguórénde jiā děi dài yìdiǎnr dōngxi.	You must bring a small gift when you go to a Chinese person's home.

CULTURAL NOTE The Polite Measure Word **Wèi** to Refer to People (II)

Notice that Eric Goodman uses **nèiwèi** instead of **nèige** to show respect when he refers to the manager's wife. You have learned this **wèi** in Lesson 11. Also distinguish **nèiwèi** (that one) from **něiwèi** (which one).

CULTURAL NOTE Using **Duō Chī/Hē Diǎnr** to Show Hospitality

Duō chī/hē diǎnr is short for **Duō chī/hē (yì)diǎnr (dōngxi)**, literally meaning "eat/drink a little more." A host will say this several times to encourage his guests to drink and eat their fill and to show his/her sincerity and hospitality. This kind of invitational expression should not be interpreted as demanding; rather, it should be seen as a warm gesture by the host.

GRAMMAR NOTE Politely Refusing Requests

The literal meaning of **yòng** is "need" as a verb. **Bú yòng, xièxie** is the best way to decline the host's offer of **Nǐ yào hē jiǔ ma** "Do you want to drink wine?", followed by a reason (e.g., **Wǒ děi kāichē** "I have to drive"). This is generally an acceptable way to politely refuse requests, although it may differ in situations and may require systematic learning. Definitely avoid saying **Wǒ bú yào** "I don't want to" in this instance as it sounds extremely rude and will make the host lose face.

Pattern Practice 1

Practice saying the following phrases.
Nǐ(de) jiā + verb phrase

Nǐ(de) jiā yǒu jǐge rén?	How many people are there in your family?
Nǐ(de) jiā yǒu shénme rén?	Who are the members of your family?
Nǐ(de) jiā zài nǎr?	Where is your home?
Nǐ(de) jiā zài Běijīng ma?	Is your home in Beijing?

Pattern Practice 2

Practice saying the following phrases.
Liǎng + measure word + noun

Wáng Mǐn yǒu liǎng gegēge.	Wang Min has two older brothers.
Wǒ yǒu liǎngge wèntí.	I have two questions.
Wǒmen yǒu liǎngjiàn dàhàode tǐxùshān.	We have two large-sized t-shirts.

Pattern Practice 3

Practice saying the following phrases.
Subject + number + **suì** + (**le**)

Wǒ èrshí suì(le).	I am twenty years old.
Wǒ bàba wǔshísìsuì(le).	My father is fifty-four years old.
Wǒ jiějie èrshísānsuì(le).	My older sister is twenty-three years old.
Wǒ dìdi shíbāsuì(le).	My younger brother is eighteen years old.

Pattern Practice 4

Practice saying the following phrases.
Noun 1 + **bǐ** + Noun 2 + stative verb

Lín Jīnglǐde nǚ'ér bǐ érzi dà.	Manager Lin's daughter is older than his son.
Zhèige cài bǐ nèige cài là.	This dish is more spicy than that one.
Wǒ tàitai bǐ wǒ máng.	My wife is busier than me.
Zhèige cānguǎnde cài bǐ nèige cānguǎn hǎochī.	The food in this restaurant tastes better than in that restaurant.

Pattern Practice 5

Practice saying the following phrases.
Subject + **děi** + verb phrase

Nǐ děi duō xiūxi.	You must rest more.
Nǐ děi duō yùndòng.	You must exercise more.
Nǐ děi shǎo chī làde.	You must eat spicy food less often.
Nǐ děi qù kàn yīsheng.	You must go to see a doctor.
Wǒ nónglì Xīnnián děi hé jiārén yìqǐ chīfàn.	I must eat with my family on Chinese New Year.

EXERCISE 1

Fill in each blank with one of the following expressions.

liǎng	jiù	bǐ	yǒu

1. A: **Qǐng wèn, nín shì Lín Jīnglǐ ma?**
   B: **Duì, wǒ _____ shì.**

2. **Lǐ Yáng, nǐ(de) jiā _____ jǐge rén?**

3. **Wǒ jiějie _____ wǒ gēge dà.**

4. **Wǒ yǒu _____ ge hǎo péngyǒu, yíge shì Měiguó rén, yíge shì Zhōngguó rén.**

EXERCISE 2
Answer each of the following questions in Chinese.

1. **Nǐ jiā zài nǎr?**
2. **Nǐ jiā yǒu jǐge rén?**
3. **Nǐ yǒu gēge, jiějie, dìdi, mèimei ma?**
4. **Nǐ gēge/jiějie/dìdi/mèimei duō dàle?**
5. **Nǐ bàba/māma duō dà niánjile?**
6. **Nǐ yǒu háizi ma? Tāmen jǐsuìle?**

EXERCISE 3
Translate the following dialogues into Chinese.

1. A: Where is your home?
   B: My home is in Beijing.
   A: How many people are there in your family?
   B: There are four people in my family: My father, mother, older sister and me.

2. A: How old are your son and daughter?
   B: My son is eight years old. He is older than my daughter. My daughter is six.

3. A: Would you like some wine?
   B: No, thank you. I need to drive.

EXERCISE 4
Task: Introduce your family by using the following patterns.

Wǒ jiā yǒu ...ge rén
Wǒ jiā yǒu ....
Wǒ jiā zài ....
Wǒ bàba/māma/gēge/jiějie/dìdi/mèimei jiào ..., tā ... suìle.

Shéi (who)	Míngzi	Niánjì (age)
bàba		
māma		
gēge		
jiějie		
dìdi		
mèimei		

LESSON 16
Geography and Weather

DIALOGUE Other Countries' Weather

Wang Min is having a casual conversation with Eric Goodman about his hometown at the student cafeteria.

Min: Gao Zhi'an, where is your home in the US?
Gāo Zhì'ān, nǐ jiā zài Měiguó shénme dìfang?
高志安，你家在美国什么地方？

Eric: My home is in Boston. I was born there and it's where I grew up.
Wǒ jiā zài Bōshìdùn, wǒ shì zài nàr chūshēng zhǎngdàde.
我家在波士顿，我是在那儿出生长大的。

Min: What is the climate like there?
Nàrde qìhòu zěnmeyàng?
那儿的气候怎么样？

Eric: Winter is both long and cold. Spring is short. Summer is not too hot. Autumn is the most comfortable season.
Dōngtiān yòu cháng yòu lěng, chūntiān hěn duǎn, xiàtiān bú tài rè, qiūtiān zuì shūfu.
冬天又长又冷，春天很短，夏天不太热，秋天最舒服。

Min: Does it snow often?
Chángcháng xiàxuě ma?
常常下雪吗？

Eric: It often snows in the winter.
Dōngtiān chángcháng xiàxuě.
冬天常常下雪。

Min: Is Boston far from New York City?
Bōshìdùn lí Niǔyuē yuǎn-bùyuǎn?
波士顿离纽约远不远？

Eric: It's close. It's only an hour by airplane and about four hours by car.
Hěn jìn, zuò fēijī zhǐ yào yíge xiǎoshí, kāichē yào chàbuduō sìge xiǎoshí.
很近，坐飞机只要一个小时，开车要差不多四个小时。

New Vocabulary

Pinyin	Chinese Character	English
Dìfang	地方	Place (n)
Bōshìdùn	波士顿	Boston
Shì...de	是...的	(Emphasizes place or time of known past action)
Nàr	那	There

New Vocabulary (cont'd)

Pinyin	Chinese Character	English
Chūshēng	出生	Born
Zhǎngdà	长大	Grow up
Qìhòu	气候	Climate
Dōngtiān	冬天	Winter season
Yòu...yòu...	又...又...	Both ... and ...
Cháng	长	Long
Lěng	冷	Cold
Chūntiān	春天	Spring season
Duǎn	短	Short
Xiàtiān	夏天	Summer season
Tài	太	Too
Rè	热	Hot
Qiūtiān	秋天	Autumn season
Chángcháng	常常	Often
Xiàxuě	下雪	Snow
Lí	离	Be distanced from
Niǔyuē	纽约	New York City; the New York state is **Niǔyuē zhōu** (state)
Yuǎn	远	Far
Jìn	近	Close, near
Zuò	坐	Take (vehicles) (lit. sit)
Fēijī	飞机	Airplane
Zhǐ	只	Only
Yào	要	Take, cost
Xiǎoshí	小时	Hour
Chàbuduō	差不多	About
Sì	四	Four

Supplementary Vocabulary

Other Common Means of Public Transportation That Go With Zuò-

Pinyin	English
Zuò gōnggòngqìchē	By bus
Zuò dìtiě	By subway
Zuò huǒchē	By train
Zuò chuán	By boat

Other Means of Transportation that Do Not Go With Zuò-

Pinyin	English
Qí zìxíngchē	By bike, ride a bike
Zǒulù	By foot, walk

Other Common Stative Verbs or Verbs to Describe Weather

Pinyin	English
Gān	Dry
Shī	Humid
Xiàyǔ	Rain

GRAMMAR NOTE The Expression **Shénme Dìfang** = "What Place"

Dìfang means "place". **Shénme dìfang** means "what place", which is pretty much interchangeable with the **nǎr** (where) you learned in Lesson 7 and helps the listener and speaker to identify the location. Examples:

Nǐ jiā zài Zhōnguó shénme dìfang? — Where is your home in China?
Gāo Zhì'ān kāichē qù shénme dìfang? — Where is Gao Zhi'an driving to?
Nǐ píngcháng xǐhuan qù shénme dìfang chīfàn? — Where do you usually like to go to eat?

GRAMMAR NOTE The Pattern **Shì ...De** = "Was [Past Tense of Verb]"

The **shì...de** pattern is used to emphasize the place or time of a known past action, such as the place or year of one's birth. Examples:

Wǒ shì zài Měiguó chūshēngde. — I was born in the US.
Wǒ shì zài Měiguó zhǎngdàde. — I grew up in the US.
Nǐ shì zài nǎr chūshēng zhǎngdàde? — Where were you born and where did you grow up?

Helpful Tips:
1. **Wǒ zài Měiguó chūshēng** or **Wǒ zài Měiguó zhǎngdà** alone are not complete sentences; the use of **shì...de** pattern in these examples is mandatory.

2. There is no **hé** (and) between the two verbs **chūshēng** and **zhǎngdà** in the sentence **Nǐ shì zài nǎr chūshēng zhǎngdàde?** ("Where were you born and where did you grow up?"). **Hé** cannot be used to connect two verbs or sentences in Chinese.

GRAMMAR NOTE Both ... and ... to Express Two Coexisting Qualities

The pattern **yòu...yòu...** is used to connect two stative verbs to express two coexisting qualities. Examples:

Bōshìdùnde dōngtiān yòu cháng yòu lěng. — The winter in Boston is long and cold.

Wǒ zuìjìn yòu máng yòu lèi.   I am busy and tired recently.
Zhérde cài yòu piányi yòu hǎochī.   The food here is cheap and tasty.

Helpful Tips:

1. The two stative verbs need be both positive or negative; you cannot mix them and have one positive and one negative. Thus, like in English, it's ungrammatical to say **Zhérde cài yòu hěn piányi yòu bù hǎochī.**

2. Do not use **hěn** in front of the stative verb. It is ungrammatical to say **Zhérde cài yòu hěn piányi yòu hěn hǎochī.**

GRAMMAR NOTE Softening Negative Meanings

In the cultural note of Lesson 8, we mentioned that when the stative verb has negative meanings, Chinese people tend to use this **bú tài** + stative verb structure to avoid directness. This structure appears in the dialogue of Lesson 16 when Eric describes the summer in Boston as **Bōshìdùnde xiàtiān bú tài rè** ("The summer in Boston is not too hot"). More examples:

Instead of saying:

Shítángde cài tài nánchīle.   The food in the dining hall is awful.
Wàimiànde dōngxi tài guìle.   The things outside are too expensive.
Wǒ jīntiān hěn bù shūfu.   I am feeling very ill today.

You say:

Shítángde cài bú tài hǎochī.   The food in the dining hall is not so tasty.
Wàimiànde dōngxi bú tài piányi.   The things outside are not so cheap.
Wǒ jīntiān bú tài shūfu.   I am not feeling well today.

GRAMMAR NOTE Describing the Weather

Notice that **xiàxuě** and **xiàyǔ** function as verbs in Chinese. **Xiàxuě** is composed of **xià** (fall) and **xuě** (snow), literally meaning "falling snow". **Xiàyǔ** is composed of **xià** (fall) and **yǔ** (rain), lit., "falling rain". The common pattern for **xiàxuě** and **xiàyǔ** is "Time Word + **xiàxuě/xiàyǔ**." Examples:

Míngtiān huì xiàyǔ.   It will rain tomorrow.
Bōshìdùnde dōngtiān chángcháng   It often snows in winter in Boston.
  xiàxuě.

If you want to say "It's snowing now," you need to say **xiàxuěle**. Likewise, **xiàyǔle** means "it's raining now."

GRAMMAR NOTE ## Distance Between Two Places Using "Far/ Near"

"Place 1 + **lí** + Place 2 + **hěn/bù** + **yuǎn/jìn**" is a pattern to describe the distance between two places. Examples:

Zhōngguó lí Měiguó hěn yuǎn.	China is far from the US.
Bōshìdùn lí Niǔyuē bù yuǎn.	Boston is not far from New York.
Lǐ Yáng jiā lí Wáng Mǐn jiā hěn jìn.	Li Yang's home is close to Wang Min's.

Hěn is a grammatical marker in this pattern and cannot be omitted.

GRAMMAR NOTE ## Means of Public Transportation "To Sit/ Take Vehicle"

You have learned the original meaning of **zuò** (to sit) in Lesson 5. In this lesson, **zuò** means "to take (vehicles)" and it needs to be followed by means of public transportation. Examples:

zuò fēijī	by airplane
zuò gōnggòngqìchē	by bus
zuò dìtiě	by subway

This pattern functions as verb or topic in a sentence. Examples:

Nǐ kéyi zuò fēijī qù Niǔyuē.	You can fly to New York City by airplane.
Nǐ xǐhuan zuò fēijī ma?	Do you like taking the airplane?
Zuò gōnggòngqìchē hěn màn.	Taking bus is slow.
Zuò fēijī qù Měiguó yào shíge xiǎoshí.	It takes ten hours to fly to America.

GRAMMAR NOTE ## The Verb **Yào** = "To Take..." Expresses Time Duration

You have learned **yào** meaning "to want" in Lesson 9. In this lesson, **yào** + time duration indicates that the time duration for the journey is very long. Compare:

Qù Niǔyuē sìge xiǎoshí.	It takes four hours to go to New York City.
Qù Niǔyuē yào sìge xiǎoshí.	The journey to New York City is so long it takes four hours to get there.
Qù Bōshìdùn shísìge xiǎoshí.	It takes fourteen hours to go to Boston.
Qù Bōshìdùn yào shísìge xiǎoshí.	The (flight) to Boston is so long that it takes fourteen hours to get there.
Qù Běijīng yíge xiǎoshí.	It takes one hour to go to Beijing.
Qù Běijīng yào yíge xiǎoshí.	The journey to Beijing is so long that it takes one hour to get there.

GRAMMAR NOTE **Using the Adverb Zhǐ = "Only"**

The adverb **zhǐ** means "only" and it needs to be put between the subject and the verb. Examples:

Zhèijiàn yīfu zhǐ yǒu zhōnghàode.	This shirt/dress is only available in medium.
Wǒ zhǐ yǒu Gāo Zhì'ānde shǒujī hàomǎ.	I only have Gao Zhi'an's cell phone number.
Wǒ zhǐ zhīdào tā xué Zhōngguó lìshǐ.	I only know that he/she studies Chinese history.

Helpful Tips:

The reason why **yào** is mandatory in the sentence **zuò fēijī zhǐ yào yíge xiǎoshí** is because **zhǐ** means "only" and it requires a verb to follow. Therefore, **yào** in this sentence does not have the implication of "long" as it does in the next sentence **kāichē yào chàbuduō sìge xiǎoshí** ("You need to drive for four hours"). This can be brought across with the inflection of your tone that signifies that the journey is very long.

GRAMMAR NOTE **The Adverb Chàbuduō = "About, Around"**

The adverb **chàbuduō** meaning "about, around" is usually followed by a numerical expression. Examples:

chàbuduō sìge xiǎoshí	about four hours
chàbuduō liùdiǎn	about six o'clock
chàbuduō shísuì	about ten years old

Helpful Tips:

Both **Zuò fēijī zhǐ yào yíge xiǎoshí** ("It takes only an hour by airplane") and **Kāichē yào chàbuduō sìge xiǎoshí** ("It takes about four hours by car") are good examples of the Topic comment structure in Chinese. **Zuò fēijī** and **kāichē** are the topics while **zhǐ yào yíge xiǎoshí** and **yào chàbuduō sìge xiǎoshí** are the comments.

Pattern Practice 1

Practice saying the following phrases.
Subject + **shì...de**

Wǒ shì zài Měiguó chūshēngde.	I was born in the US.
Tā shì zài Zhōngguó zhǎngdàde.	He/She grew up in China.
Nǐde nǚ'ér shì zài nǎr chūshēngde?	Where was your daughter born?
Nǐde érzi shì zài nǎr zhǎngdàde?	Where did your son grow up?
Nǐ shì zài nǎr chūshēng zhǎngdà de?	Where were you born (and where) did you grow up?

Pattern Practice 2

Practice saying the following phrases.
Subject + **yòu** + stative verb 1 + **yòu** + stative verb 2

Niǔyuēde dōngtiān yòu cháng yòu lěng.	The winter in New York City is long and cold.
Tā zuìjìn yòu máng yòu lèi.	He/She is busy and tired recently.
Zhèijiàn yīfu yòu héshì yòu shūfu.	This shirt/dress fits well and is comfortable.
Wǒmen xuéxiào shítángde cài yòu piányi yòu hǎochī.	The food in our school's dining hall is cheap and tasty.

Pattern Practice 3

Practice saying the following phrases.
Place 1 + **lí** + Place 2 + **hěn/bù** + **yuǎn/jìn**

Měiguó lí Zhōngguó hěn yuǎn.	The US is far from China.
Bōshìdùn lí Niǔyuē bù yuǎn.	Boston is not far from New York City.
Wǒ jiā lí Qīnghuá Dàxué bù yuǎn.	My home is not far from Tsinghua University.

Pattern Practice 4

Practice saying the following phrases.
Topic + **yào** + time duration

Qù Bōshìdùn yào sānge xiǎoshí.	It takes three hours to go to Boston.
Qù Niǔyuē yào liùge xiǎoshí.	It takes six hours to go to New York City.
Kāichē qù Běijīng yào shíge xiǎoshí.	It takes ten hours to go to Beijing by car.
Tā chīfàn yào liǎngge xiǎoshí.	He/she takes two hours to finish eating.

Pattern Practice 5

Practice saying the following phrases.
Subject + **zhǐ** (only) + verb phrase

Wǒmen zhǐ yǒu shuǐ hé kāfēi.	We have only water and coffee.
Wǒ zhǐ tōngzhīle Lín Jīnglǐ.	I only informed Manager Lin.
Wǒ zhǐ zhīdào tā xìng Chén.	I only know that his/her family name is Chen.
Tā zhǐ zài xuéxiàode shítáng chīfàn, bú qù wàimiànde cānguǎn.	He/She only eats at the school's dining halls; he/she doesn't go to the outside restaurants (to eat).

Pattern Practice 6

Chàbuduō (about) + numerical expression

Tāde érzi jīnnián chàbuduō sìsuìle.	His/Her son is about four years old this year.
Xiànzài chàbuduō shàngwǔ jiǔdiǎn.	Now it's about 9 am.
Qù Niǔyuē chàbuduō wǔge xiǎoshí.	It takes about five hours to go to New York City.
Wǒde nǚ'ér jīnnián chàbuduō shíbāsuìle.	My daughter is about eighteen years old this year.

Pattern Practice 7

Zuò + means of transportation = "by transportation" as verb

Nǐ xǐhuan zuò fēijī ma?	Do you like to take the airplane?
Wǒ jīntiān bú tài xiǎng zuò dìtiě.	I don't really want to take the subway today.
Nǐ kéyǐ zuò gōnggòngqìchē qù Qīnghuá Dàxué.	You can take the bus to Tsinghua University.

Zuò + means of transportation = "by transportation" as topic

Zuò fēijī bǐjiào kuài.	Taking the airplane is faster.
Zuò gōnggòngqìchē hěn màn.	Taking the bus is slow.
Zài Niǔyuē zuò dìtiě tǐng guìde.	It's pretty expensive to take the subway in New York City.

EXERCISE 1

Fill in each blank with one of the following expressions.

lí	zuò	yào	de

1. **Zuò fēijī _____ shíge xiǎoshí. Tài yuǎn le.**

2. **Nǐ jiā _____ xuéxiào yuǎn-bùyuǎn?**

3. **Wǒ shì zài Táiwān chūshēng zhǎngdà _____.**

4. **Wǒ bú tài xǐhuan _____ gōnggòngqìchē. Tài mànle.**

EXERCISE 2
Answer each of the following questions in Chinese.
1. **Nǐ shì zài nàr chūshēng zhǎngdàde?**
2. **Nǐ jiā zài shénme dìfang?**
3. **Nàrde qìhòu zěnmeyàng?**
4. **Nàr xiàxuě ma?**

EXERCISE 3
Translate the following dialogues into Chinese.

1. A: Where is your home in China?
   B: My home is in Tianjin (**Tiānjīn**).
   A: Is Tianjin far from Beijing?
   B: It's not far. It takes about an hour by train.

2. A: What is the climate like in New York City?
   B: The winter is long and cold. The summer is not too hot.
   A: How about the autumn?
   B: I like the autumn the most—it's pretty (**piàoliang**).

3. A: Does it snow in Beijing?
   B: Yes, it snows frequently in the winter. How about Boston?
   A: It snows frequently too, but I think Boston is colder than Beijing.

EXERCISE 4
Role Playing
You are on a flight from New York to Shanghai. It is your first time to visit China. You have observed that the person seated beside you is a local Chinese[1]. Strike up a conversation in Chinese by asking: (1) What is his/her name? (2) Where did he/she grow up? (3) Does he/she know what the climate is like in Shanghai now? (4) Is Shanghai far from Beijing? (5) How long does it take to go to Beijing from Shanghai by airplane?

---

1 Culturally, not every Chinese-looking person may be a Chinese from China. If you're unsure, it's always safest to ask their country of origin and if they speak Chinese before asking them these questions.

LESSON 17
Traveling

Li Yang and Eric Goodman are having lunch. Eric mentions to Li Yang his plan for the spring break.

Eric:	Hey, Li Yang, do you speak Cantonese?
	Èh, Lǐ Yáng, nǐ huì shuō Guǎngdōnghuà ma?
	唉，李洋，你会说广东话吗？
Yang:	I don't.
	Wǒ bú huì.
	我不会。
Eric:	I want to go to Hong Kong and Taiwan during spring break.
	Wǒ chūnjià xiǎng qù Xiānggǎng hé Táiwān.
	我春假想去香港和台湾。
Yang:	I have been to Hong Kong. It's very interesting. I have never been to Taiwan. I've heard that the Taiwanese cuisine is delicious and the scenery is beautiful.
	Xiānggǎng wǒ qùguo, hěn yǒuyìsi. Wǒ méi qùguo Táiwān, tīngshuō Táiwān cài hěn hǎochī, fēngjǐng yě hěn piàoliang.
	香港我去过，很有意思。我没去过台湾，听说台湾菜很好吃，风景也很漂亮 。
Eric:	How long does it take from Beijing to Hong Kong by airplane?
	Cóng Běijīng dào Xiānggǎng zuò fēijī yào duōcháng shíjiān?
	从北京到香港坐飞机要多长时间？
Yang:	I assume it's about four hours.
	Chàbuduō sìge xiǎoshí ba.
	差不多四个小时吧。
Eric:	Okay. I have class now and need to go. Talk to you later.
	En. Wǒ yǒu kè, děi zǒule, zài liáo.
	嗯。我有课，得走了，再聊。
Yang:	Okay, talk to you later.
	Hǎo, zài liáo.
	好，再聊。

New Vocabulary

Pinyin	Chinese Character	English
Huì	会	Can, know how to, able to (indicates capability)
Shuō	说	Speak
Guǎngdōnghuà	广东话	Cantonese language

New Vocabulary (cont'd)

Pinyin	Chinese Character	English
Huì	会	Can, know how to, able to (indicates capability)
Shuō	说	Speak
Guǎngdōnghuà	广东话	Cantonese language
Chūnjià*	春假	Spring break—usually at the end of March or the beginning of April. **Hánjià**: winter break; **shǔjià**: summer break
Xiānggǎng	香港	Hong Kong
Táiwān	台湾	Taiwan
-Guo	过	(Indicates personal experience)
Yǒuyìsi	有意思	Interesting
Tīngshuō	听说	Heard
Fēngjǐng	风景	Scenery
Piàoliang	漂亮	Beautiful, pretty
Cóng... dào...	从...到...	From ... to ...
Duō-	多	How
Shíjiān	时间	Time (n)
Duōcháng shíjiān	多长时间	How long
Kè	课	Class
Děi	得	Need to
Zǒu	走	Go, leave
Zài	再	Again, a homonym with **zài** but written with different Chinese characters.
Liáo	聊	Chat

Supplementary Vocabulary   Languages

Pinyin	English
Yīngwén	English
Fǎwén	French
Déwén	German
Rìwén	Japanese
Hánwén	Korean
Pútáoyáwén	Portuguese
Éwén	Russian
Xībānyáwén	Spanish
Tàiwén	Thai
Yuènánwén	Vietnamese

Other Common Dialects in China

Pinyin	English
Húnánhuà	Hunan dialect
Kèjiāhuà	Hakka dialect
Mǐnnánhuà*	Southern Min dialect
Sìchuānhuà	Sichuan dialect
Shāndōnghuà	Shandong dialect
Shànghǎihuà	Shanghai dialect

*The other related terms are **Fújiànhuà** (Hokkien dialect) or **Cháozhōuhuà** (Teochew dialect).

GRAMMAR NOTE The Auxiliary Verb **Huì** = Ability to Do Something

In this lesson, **huì** needs to be followed by a verb phrase. Examples:

Qǐng wèn, nǐ huì shuō Yīngwén ma?	Excuse me, do you speak English?
Wǒ huì shuō Zhōngwén.	I can speak Chinese.
Nǐ huì yóuyǒng ma?	Do you know how to swim?

The negation of **huì** is **bú huì**. Examples:

Wǒ bú huì shuō Guǎngdōnghuà.	I don't speak Cantonese.
Tā bú huì shuō Zhōngwén.	He/She doesn't speak Chinese.

GRAMMAR NOTE **Shuō** + a Language = "Speak a Language"

Shuō is the verb to use when you want to say "speak". Examples:

Wǒ huì shuō Zhōngwén.	I can speak Chinese.
Lǐ Yáng huì shuō Hánwén.	Li Yang can speak Korean.
Wáng Mǐn huì shuō Xībānyáwén.	Wang Min can speak Spanish.

Helpful Tips:

Chinese people often insert the word **yìdiǎnr** (a little) between **shuō** and "a language", e.g., **Wǒ huì shuō yìdiǎnr Yīngyǔ** ("I speak a little English.") even if they are fluent, in order to remain humble and not showcase their ability too much.

GRAMMAR NOTE The Verb + **Guo** = Past Experiences

The structure "verb + **guo**" indicates experiences in the past. Examples:

Wǒ qùguo Xiānggǎng.	I have been to Hong Kong.
Gāo Zhì'ān hēguo Zhōngguó jiǔ.	Gao Zhi'an has drunk Chinese wine before.

Nǐ chīguo Táiwān cài ma?	Have you ever eaten Taiwanese cuisine before?

To negate, put **méi** in front of verb + **guo**. Examples:

Wǒ méi qùguo Xiānggǎng.	I have never been to Hong Kong.
Gāo Zhì'ān méi hēguo Zhōngguó jiǔ.	Gao Zhi'an has never drunk Chinese wine.
Wǒmen méi chīguo Táiwān cài.	We've never eaten Taiwanese cuisine before.

Helpful Tip:
"Verb + **le**" indicates completion whereas "Verb + **guo**" indicates experience.

GRAMMAR NOTE   The Word "**Tīngshuō**" = "Heard"

The verb **tīngshuō** needs to be followed by a statement. Examples:

Wǒ tīngshuō Táiwān cài hěn hǎochī.	I heard that Taiwanese cuisine is delicious.
Wǒ tīngshuō xué Zhōngwén hěn yǒuyìsi.	I heard that learning Chinese is interesting.
Wáng Mǐn tīngshuō Bōshìdùnde dōngtiān yòu cháng yòu lěng.	Wang Min heard that the winter in Boston is long and cold.

GRAMMAR NOTE   The Pattern **Cóng... Dào...** = "From...to..."

The pattern **cóng... dào...** can connect two place words or time words. Examples:

Cóng Běijīng dào Xiānggǎng	from Beijing to Hong Kong
Cóng Měiguó dào Zhōngguó	from US to China
Cóng jiǔdiǎn dào shíyīdiǎn	from 9 o'clock to 11 o'clock

GRAMMAR NOTE   The Question Phrase **Duōcháng Shíjiān** ="How Long"

Duō is a question word meaning "how." **Cháng** means "long." **Shíjiān** means "time." **Duōcháng shíjiān** is a question phrase meaning "how long" or "how much time." Examples:

Cóng Běijīng dào Xiānggǎng zuò fēijī yào duōcháng shíjiān?	How long does it take from Beijing to Hong Kong by airplane?
Cóng zhèr dào nàr yào duōcháng shíjiān?	How long does it take from here to there?
Cóng Bōshìdùn dào Niǔyuē kāichē yào duōcháng shíjiān?	How long does it take from Boston to New York City by car?

CULTURAL NOTE	Politely Excusing Yourself When Departing Early

Wǒ děi zǒule ("I need to go") is a useful expression to politely take an early departure in a conversation. To make it even more polite, you can add **duìbuqǐ** ("sorry") in the front and say **Duìbuqǐ, wǒ děi zǒule** ("Sorry, I have to go"). If you have a class, you can say **Duìbuqǐ, wǒ yǒu kè, děi zǒule.** If you don't want to specify the reason, you can simply say **Duìbuqǐ, wǒ yǒu shí(r), děi zǒule** ("Sorry, I have things to attend to. I need to go"). The **le** at the end of the sentence indicates a change of state (equivalent to "I have to go already" or "I have to go now").

CULTURAL NOTE	The Phrase **Zài Liáo** = "Talk to You Later"

You learned the expression **zàijiàn** to mean "goodbye." **Zài liáo** is another useful expression between acquaintances meaning "talk to you later." Notice that the adverb **zài** (again) needs to precede the verb **liáo** (chat). It is ungrammatical to say **liáo zài.**

Pattern Practice 1

Practice saying the following phrases
Subject + **huì** + verb phrase

Wǒ huì shuō Yīngwén.	I can speak English.
Gāo Zhì'ān huì shuō Zhōngwén.	Gao Zhi'an can speak Chinese.
Lǐ Yáng huì yóuyǒng.	Li Yang knows how to swim.
Wáng Mǐn bú huì kāichē.	Wang Min doesn't know how to drive.

Pattern Practice 2

Practice saying the following phrases
Subject + verb + **guo** + noun phrase

Wǒ qùguo Xiānggǎng.	I have been to Hong Kong.
Tā qùguo Táiwān.	He/She has been to Taiwan.
Nǐ chīguo Táiwān cài ma?	Have you ever had Taiwanese cuisine before?
Nǐ chīguo yuèbǐng ma?	Have you ever had mooncakes before?
Nǐ hēguo jiǔ ma?	Have you had alcohol before?

Pattern Practice 3

Practice saying the following phrases
Subject + **tīngshuō** + sentence

Wǒ tīngshuō Táiwān cài hěn hǎochī.	I've heard that Taiwanese cuisine is delicious.
Wǒ tīngshuō xué Zhōngwén hěn nán.	I've heard that learning Chinese is hard.
Wǒ tīngshuō Zhāng Lǎoshī zuìjìn yǒuyìdiǎnr bù shūfu.	I've heard that Professor Zhang hasn't been feeling well recently.
Wáng Mǐn tīngshuō Bōshìdùnde dōngtiān yòu cháng yòu lěng.	Wang Min heard that the winter in Boston is both long and cold.

Pattern Practice 4

Practice saying the following phrases.
Cóng... dào...

cóng Běijīng dào Xiānggǎng	from Beijing to Hong Kong
cóng Měiguó dào Zhōngguó	from the US to China
cóng Niǔyuē dào Bōshìdùn	from New York City to Boston
cóng jiǔdiǎn dào shíyīdiǎn	from 9 o'clock to 11 o'clock
cóng yùndòng zhōngxīn dào yóuyǒngguǎn	from the sports center to the swimming complex

Pattern Practice 5

Practice saying the following phrases.
Topic + **yào** + **duōcháng shíjiān**

Cóng Niǔyuē dào Bōshìdùn zuò fēijī yào duōcháng shíjiān?	How long does it take from New York City to Boston by airplane?
Cóng Niǔyuē dào Bōshìdùn kāichē yào duōcháng shíjiān?	How long does it take from New York City to Boston by car?
Cóng zhèr dào nàr zuò dìtiě yào duōcháng shíjiān?	How long does it take from here to there by subway?
Cóng zhèr dào nàr zǒulù yào duōcháng shíjiān?	How long does it take to walk from here to there?

EXERCISE 1

Fill in each blank with one of the following expressions.

huì	děi	tīngshuō	dào

1. Qǐng wèn, nǐ _____ shuō Guǎngdōnghuà ma?

2. Wǒ _____ Táiwān cài hěn hǎochī, nǐ chīguo ma?

3. Cóng Běijīng _____ Shànghǎi zuò fēijī yào jǐge xiǎoshí?

4. Wǒ yǒu shír, _____ zǒule.

EXERCISE 2
Answer each of the following questions in Chinese.

1. Nǐ huì shuō shénme yǔyán (language)?
2. Nǐ qùguo Xiānggǎng hé Táiwān ma?
3. Nǐ xǐhuan qù nǎr gòuwù?
4. Cóng nǐ jiā dào Běijīng zuò fēijī yào duōcháng shíjiān?

EXERCISE 3
Translate the following dialogues into Chinese.

1. A: Excuse me, do you speak English?
   B: I speak a little English. Do you speak Chinese?
   A: I don't.

2. A: Have you been to New York City before?
   B: Yes, I went there in June this year. It's very interesting.
   A: Have you been to Boston?
   B: No, I have never been to Boston.

3. A: I heard that San Francisco (Jiùjīnshān) is far.
   B: How long does it take from Beijing to San Francisco by airplane?
   A: It takes about twelve hours.

EXERCISE 4
Task: Below are a few Chinese cities. Search online for the answers to how long the journey will take.

cóng	dào	zuò...	yào duōcháng shíjiān?
Běijīng	Shànghǎi	zuò fēijī	
Běijīng	Tiānjīn	kāichē	
Xiānggǎng	Táiběi	zuò fēijī	
Xiānggǎng	Shēnzhèn	kāichē	
Xiānggǎng	Guǎngzhōu	zuò huǒchē	
Shànghǎi	Nánjīng	zuò huǒchē	

LESSON 18
Arranging a Ride to the Airport

DIALOGUE Calling A Taxi Company

Eric Goodman is trying to book a taxi to take him to the airport.

Receptionist:	Beijing Yinjian Taxi Company, how can I help you?
	Wéi, Běijīng Yínjiàn Chūzūqìchē Gōngsī, nín hǎo.
	喂，北京银建出租汽车公司，您好。
Eric:	Hello, I would like a car to take me to the Capital Airport tomorrow.
	Nǐ hǎo. Wǒ míngtiān yào yíliàng chē qù Shǒudū Jīchǎng.
	你好。我明天要一辆车去首都机场。
Receptionist:	No problem. What is your last name, Sir?
	Méi wèntí. Xiānsheng, nín guìxìng?
	没问题。先生，您贵姓？
Eric:	My last name is Gao.
	Wǒ xìng Gāo.
	我姓高。
Receptionist:	What time tomorrow, Mr. Gao?
	Gāo Xiānsheng, míngtiān jǐdiǎn?
	高先生，明天几点？
Eric:	2 pm.
	Xiàwǔ liǎngdiǎn.
	下午两点。
Receptionist:	Where would you like to be picked up?
	Zài shénme dìfang jiē nín?
	在什么地方接您？
Eric:	At the international student building of Tsinghua University. Excuse me, how long is the trip, and how much will it cost?
	Qīnghuá Dàxué liúxuéshēng lóu. Qǐng wèn, dào jīchǎng yào duōcháng shíjiān, duōshǎo qián?
	清华大学留学生楼。请问，到机场要多长时间、多少钱？
Receptionist:	It takes approximately an hour from Tsinghua University to the airport and it costs about 120 RMB. Your telephone number is …
	Cóng Qīnghuá Dàxué dào jīchǎng chàbuduō yào yíge xiǎoshí, yìbǎi èrshíkuài qián zuǒyòu. Nínde diànhuà shì…
	从清华大学到机场差不多要一个小时，120块钱左右。您的电话是…
Eric:	My cell phone number is 139-2227-6688.
	Wǒde shǒujī hàomǎ shì 139-2227-6688.
	我的手机号码是 139-2227-6688。

Receptionist:	I am sorry. Could you please say it again?
	Duìbuqǐ, qǐng nín zài shuō yíbiàn.
	对不起，请您再说一遍。
Eric:	139-2227-6688.
	139-2227-6688.
	139-2227-6688。
Receptionist:	Great. We'll pick you up tomorrow on time.
	Hǎo, míngtiān huì zhǔnshí qù jiē nín.
	好，明天会准时去接您。
Eric:	Thank you.
	Xièxie.
	谢谢。
Receptionist:	Thank you, Sir. Goodbye.
	Xièxie nín, zàijiàn.
	谢谢您，再见。
Eric:	Bye.
	Zàijiàn.
	再见。

New Vocabulary

Pinyin	Chinese Character	English
Yínjiàn	银建	(name of a taxi company in Beijing)
Chūzūqìchē	出租汽车	Taxi (lit., rental car, sedan)
Gōngsī	公司	Company
Liàng	辆	(Measure word for ground vehicles)
Chē	车	Car
Shǒudū	首都	Capital city
Jīchǎng	机场	Airport
Shǒudū Jīchǎng	首都机场	Beijing Capital International Airport
Méi wèntí	没问题	"No problem"
Nín guìxìng	您贵姓	"What is your honorable last name"
Jiē	接	Pick up
Liúxuéshēng	留学生	International student
Lóu	楼	Hall, building
Duōshǎo	多少	How much, how many
Qián	钱	Money
Duōshǎo qián	多少钱	How much money
-Bǎi	百	Hundred
Kuài	块	(Measure word for money)
Zuǒyòu	左右	About
Duìbuqǐ	对不起	"I am sorry"
Shuō	说	Say
Biàn	遍	(Measure word for time – as in "one more time")
Zhǔnshí	准时	On time, punctual

Supplementary Vocabulary

Official Currencies in Mainland China, Taiwan, and Hong Kong

Pinyin	English	Abbreviations	Used in
Gǎngbì	Hong Kong RMB	HKD	Hong Kong
Rénmínbì	Reminbi (Chinese Yuan)	RMB	Mainland China
Xīntáibì	New Taiwan Dollar	TWD	Taiwan

GRAMMAR NOTE   The Measure Word **Liàng** for Ground Vehicles

Liàng is a measure word for ground vehicles. Examples:

yíliàng gōnggòngqìchē	one public bus
liǎngliàng huǒchē	two trains
sānliàng zìxíngchē	three bikes

Helpful Tip:

You probably already noticed that all the ground transportation mentioned above end with **chē**, which literally means "car." The measure word **liàng** cannot be used for **chuán** (boat – this would be **sōu**) or **fēijī** (airplane – this would be **jià**), words which do not end with **chē**.

GRAMMAR NOTE   The Verb **Yào** = "Want" to Order or Purchase

You have learned **yào** as a verb in Lesson 11 meaning "want or ask" and in Lesson 16 meaning "take" with the implication that the time duration is long. Examples:

Lín Jīnglǐ yào wǒ gěi tā dǎ diànhuà.	Manager Lin asked me to give him a call.
Qù Niǔyuē zuò fēijī yào yíge xiǎoshí.	It takes an hour to go to New York City by airplane.

In this lesson, **yào** functions as a verb meaning "want" in the sense of "ordering" or "purchasing." It needs to be followed by a noun phrase. Examples:

Wǒ míngtiān yào yíliàng chē.	I want (to reserve) a car tomorrow.
Wǒ yào zhèijiàn yīfu.	I want (to purchase) this shirt/dress.
Wǒ yào zhèige cài.	I want (to order) this dish.

This **yào** is frequently used when shopping, ordering food and making reservations.

GRAMMAR NOTE

Using the Expression **Duōsho Qián** to ask for Price

The expression **duōshǎo qián** means "how much money" and the typical pattern to ask for price is "Topic + **duōshǎo qián**." Examples:

Zhèige duōshǎo qián?	How much is this?
Zhèijiàn yīfu duōshǎo qián?	How much is this shirt/dress?
Cóng zhèr dào Xiānggǎng zuò fēijī duōshǎo qián?	How much does it cost from here to Hong Kong by airplane?

Yào can be inserted between the topic and **duōshǎo qián** with the implication that the item may not be cheap. Compare:

Zhèige duōshǎo qián?	How much is this? (general inquiry)
Zhèige yào duōshǎo qián?	How much is this? (with the implication that **zhèige** may not be cheap.)
Zhèijiàn yīfu duōshǎo qián?	How much is this shirt/dress? (general inquiry)
Zhèijiàn yīfu yào duōshǎo qián?	How much is this shirt/dress? (with the implication that **zhèijiàn yīfu** may not be cheap.)

To respond, follow the "Topic + number + **kuài qián**" pattern. **Kuài** is the measure word for **qián** (money). Examples:

Zhèige wǔkuài qián.	This one costs five RMB.
Zhèijiàn yīfu liùshíkuài qián.	This shirt/dress costs sixty RMB.
Cóng zhèr dào jīchǎng zuò chūzūqìchē yìbǎi èrshíkuài qián.	It costs one hundred and twenty RMB from here to the airport by taxi.

Similarly, you can insert **yào** between the topic and the number + **kuài qián** with the implication that the amount is not cheap. Compare:

Zhèige wǔkuài qián.	This one costs five RMB. (general statement)
Zhèige yào wǔkuài qián.	This one costs five RMB! ("It is not cheap" is implied).
Zhèijiàn yīfu liùshíkuài qián.	This shirt/dress costs sixty RMB. (general statement)
Zhèijiàn yīfu yào liùshíkuài qián.	This shirt/dress costs sixty RMB! ("This is not cheap" is implied.)

Helpful Tip:
Colloquially, **qián** can be omitted but **kuài** is always required. It is ungrammatical to follow the number with **qián**, lit. "five money" or "sixty money".

wǔkuài = **wǔkuài qián**	five RMB
liùshíkuài = **liùshíkuài qián**	sixty RMB
yìbǎi èrshíkuài = **yìbǎi èrshíkuài qián**	one hundred and twenty RMB

GRAMMAR NOTE
Using the Word **Zuǒyòu** to Express Approximation
In Lesson 16 you learned **chàbuduō** + numerical expression to mean "about..." Examples:

chàbuduō sìge xiǎoshí	about four hours
chàbuduō liùdiǎn	about six o'clock
chàbuduō shísuì	about ten years old

In this lesson, you learn another way to express approximation: numerical expression + **zuǒyòu**. Examples:

sìge xiǎoshí zuǒyòu.	about four hours
liùdiǎn zuǒyòu	about six o'clock
shísuì zuǒyòu	about ten years old

Remember, **chàbuduō** goes before the numerical expression while **zuǒyòu** needs to be put after the numerical expression.

CULTURAL NOTE   "What's Your Honorable Last Name?"
You have learned the general expression **Nǐ jiào shénme míngzi** ("What is your name?") in Lesson 4 to inquire about someone's name. In a formal occasion, the idiomatic expression **Nín guìxìng** is preferred. The literal meaning of **Nín guìxìng** is "What's your honorable last name?" To respond, you can say **Wǒ xìng** + last name or **Bì xìng** + last name. Once you know someone's last name, you can address him/her appropriately using his/her title, such as **Gāo Xiānsheng** (Mr. Gao), **Lín Jīnglǐ** (Manager Lin), or **Zhāng Lǎoshī** (Professor Zhang).

Helpful Tips:
Avoid saying **Nǐ guìxìng** as the polite word **guì** does not match well with the general pronoun **nǐ**.

CULTURAL NOTE

Asking Someone to Repeat with **Duìbuqǐ, qǐng nín zài shuō yíbiàn**

If someone speaks too fast and you would like him/her to repeat, **Duìbuqǐ, qǐng nín zài shuō yíbiàn** is a sophisticated expression to use. **Duìbuqǐ** means "sorry," **shuō** means "say," and **biàn** is a measure word for "time." The sentence **qǐng nín zài shuō yíbiàn** is literally "Please you again say one more time"; that is, "Could you please say it again?" Notice that as in **zài liáo** ("talk to you later") and **zàijiàn** ("goodbye"), **zài** needs to be placed before the verb phrase **shuō yíbiàn**.

Helpful Tips:

When someone says **duìbuqǐ**, you can say **méi guānxi** or **méi shí(r)** to mean "that's okay" or "not a problem."

Pattern Practice 1

Practice saying the following phrases.
Subject + **yào** + noun phrase

Wǒ míngtiān yào yíliàng chē.	I want (to reserve) a car tomorrow.
Wǒ yào nèijiàn yīfu.	I want (to purchase) that shirt/dress.
Wǒ yào zhèige cài.	I want (to order) this dish.
Wǒ yào zhèixiē yào.	I want (to purchase) these medicines.
Wǒ yào yíge yuèbǐng.	I want (to purchase) one mooncake.

Pattern Practice 2

Practice saying the following phrases.
Topic + **duōshǎo qián**

Zhèige duōshǎo qián?	How much is this?
Nèijiàn yīfu duōshǎo qián?	How much is that shirt/dress?
Yíge zòngzi duōshǎo qián?	How much is one glutinous rice dumpling?
Cóng zhèr dào Xiānggǎng zuò fēijī duōshǎo qián?	How much does it cost from here to Hong Kong by airplane?
Cóng zhèr dào jīchǎng zuò chūzūqìchē duōshǎo qián?	How much does it cost from here to the airport by taxi?

Pattern Practice 3

Practice saying the following phrases.
Number + **kuài** + **qián**

wǔkuài qián	five RMB
shíkuài qián	ten RMB
èrshíkuài qián	twenty RMB
yìbǎikuài qián	one hundred RMB
yìbǎi èrshíkuài qián	one hundred and twenty RMB

Pattern Practice 4

Practice saying the following phrases.
Topic + **yào** + number + **kuài qián**

Zhèige yào wǔkuài qián.	This one costs five RMB.
Nèijiàn yīfu yào yìbǎikuài qián.	That shirt/dress costs one hundred RMB.
Zhèige yuèbǐng yào èrshíkuài qián.	This mooncake costs twenty RMB.
Cóng zhèr dào jīchǎng zuò chūzūqìchē yào yìbǎi èrshíkuài qián.	It costs one hundred and twenty RMB from here to the airport by taxi.

Pattern Practice 5

Numerical expression + **zuǒyòu**

Zhèige shíkuài qián zuǒyòu.	This one is about ten RMB.
Tā jīnnián sānshísuì zuǒyòu.	He/She is about thirty years old.
Wǒ míngtiān sìdiǎn zuǒyòu qù dǎ lánqiú.	I am going to play basketball tomorrow at about 4 o'clock.
Wǒ wǔdiǎn zuǒyòu gěi nǐ dǎ diànhuà.	I will call you at about 5 o'clock.

EXERCISE 1

Fill in each blank with one of the following expressions.

zài	qián	wéi	guìxìng

1. (On the phone)
   A: _____, nín hǎo.
   B: Nín hǎo. Qǐng wèn, Wáng Jīnglǐ zài ma?

2. A: Xiáojie, nín _____?
   B: Wǒ xìng Hé.

3. Duìbuqǐ, qǐng nín _____ shuō yíbiàn.

4. A: Zhèige duōshǎo _____?
   B: Shíkuài.

EXERCISE 2

Answer each of the following questions in Chinese.

1. Nín guìxìng?
2. Cóng nǐ jiā dào jīchǎng yào duōcháng shíjiān?
3. Cóng nǐ jiā dào jīchǎng zuò chūzūqìchē yào duōshǎo qián?

EXERCISE 3

Translate the following dialogues into Chinese.

1. (On the phone)
   A: Beijing Taxi Company, how can I help you?
   B: I'd like a taxi to the airport tomorrow.
   A: No problem. What is your (honorable) family name?
   B: My family name is Wu (Wú).

2. A: Mr. Wu, when would you like to be picked up?
   B: 3 pm.
   A: Where should we pick you up?
   B: At the international student building of Peking University.

3. A: What is your cell phone number?
   B: My cell phone number is 138-1166-5757.
   A: Great. We will pick you up on time tomorrow.
   B: Thank you.
   A: Thank you for calling.

4. A: I am sorry.
   B: That's okay.

EXERCISE 4

Task: You are calling a taxi company to arrange a ride to the airport. Inquire about the following information.
1. How much does it cost?
2. How long does it take?
3. Confirm the pick-up time and location.
4. Confirm the telephone number you can be reached at.

LESSON 19
Farewell

Eric Goodman is going back to the US tomorrow. His friends, Li Yang and Wang Min, invite him for a farewell dinner.

Eric:	Li Yang, Wang Min, thank you for treating me to a meal.
	Lǐ Yáng, Wáng Mǐn, xièxie nǐmen qǐng wǒ chīfàn.
	李洋，王敏，谢谢你们请我吃饭。
Yang:	You are welcome. Time passes really fast. You are going back to the US tomorrow.
	Bié kèqi. Shíjiān zhēn kuài, nǐ míngtiān jiù yào huí Měiguóle.
	别客气。时间真快，你明天就要回美国了。
Eric:	Yes. I remember I came just last July, and I am leaving tomorrow.
	En, wǒ jìde qùnián qīyuè gāng lái, míngtiān jiù yào zǒule.
	嗯，我记得去年七月刚来，明天就要走了。
Min:	Your Chinese has improved a lot.
	Nǐde Zhōngwén yuèláiyuè hǎole.
	你的中文越来越好了。
Eric:	No, no. I've learned a lot this past year.
	Náli, náli. Wǒ zhè yīnián xuéle hěn duō.
	哪里，哪里。我这一年学了很多。
Yang:	Do you want us to send you off at the airport tomorrow?
	Míngtiān yào-búyào sòng nǐ qù jīchǎng?
	明天要不要送你去机场？
Eric:	No, thank you. I've already reserved a taxi.
	Bú yòng, xièxie. Wǒ yǐjīng yàole yíliàng chūzūqìchē.
	不用，谢谢。我已经要了一辆出租汽车。
Min:	Okay, then let's keep in touch via email.
	Hǎo, nà wǒmen xiě diànzǐ yóujiàn bǎochí liánluò.
	好，那我们写电子邮件保持联络。
Eric:	Absolutely (lit., Yes, stay in touch)!
	En, bǎochí liánluò!
	嗯，保持联络！

New Vocabulary

Pinyin	Chinese Character	English
Qǐng	请	Invite, or the person is paying for you
Zhēn	真	Really
Kuài	快	Fast, quick
Jiù	就	Earlier than expected
Huí	回	Return, go back
Jìde	记得	Remember
Qùnián	去年	Last year
Gāng	刚	Just
Zhè yīnián	这一年	This year
Hěn duō	很多	Many, a lot
Sòng	送	Send off
Yǐjīng	已经	Already
Xiě	写	Write
Diànzǐ	电子	Electronic
Yóujiàn	邮件	Mail
Diànzǐ yóujiàn	电子邮件	Email
Bǎochí	保持	Keep, maintain
Liánluò	联络	Contact
Bǎochí liánluò	保持联络	"Stay in touch"

Supplementary Vocabulary   Common Treats between Friends

Pinyin	English
Chàng KTV	Sing karaoke (go to karaoke)
Hē kāfēi	Drink coffee
Hē chá	Drink tea
Kàn diànyǐng	See a movie

Common Farewell Expressions

Pinyin	English
Yílùshùnfēng	Have a smooth trip! (lit. "all way smooth wind")
Yílùpíng'ān	Have a safe trip! (lit. "all way safe")
Bǎozhòng	Take care!

Common Chatting Apps

Pinyin	English
Wēixìn	WeChat (dominant chatting app in Mainland China)
LINE	LINE (widely used in Taiwan)
FireChat	FireChat (popular in Hong Kong)
WhatsApp	WhatsApp (also popular in Hong Kong)

GRAMMAR NOTE Using the Verb **Qǐng** for Invitation

The verb **qǐng** means "invite" and its typical pattern is "Subject 1 + **qǐng** + Subject 2 + verb phrase." Examples:

Wǒ míngtiān qǐng nǐ hē kāfēi.	I will treat you to a cup of coffee tomorrow.
Lǐ Yáng hé Wáng Mǐn qǐng Gāo Zhì'ān chī wǎnfàn.	Li Yang and Wang Min are inviting Gao Zhi'an to dinner.
Nǐ míngtiān yǒu-méiyou shíjiān? Wǒ qǐng nǐ kàn diànyǐng.	Do you have time tomorrow? Let me treat you to a movie.

Helpful Tip:

If you want to say "my treat," it's **Wǒ qǐng nǐ** or **Wǒ qǐngkè**. If you're not sure if it's a treat, just offer to pay when the time comes. If your friend repeats the above statements, then you will not need to pay. It's also important, culturally speaking, to insist on paying for your share before graciously accepting the treat (and promising a future treat).

GRAMMAR NOTE The Intensifier Adverb **Zhēn** = "Really!"

Zhēn means "really" and is often followed by a stative verb to show it is an exclamation, i.e., "This burger is really tasty!" Examples:

Zhōngwén zhēn nán.	The Chinese language is really hard.
Zhōngguó zhēn yuǎn.	China is really far away.
Zhèige cānguǎnde cài zhēn hǎochī.	The food in this restaurant is really tasty.

GRAMMAR NOTE The Adverb **Jiù** = "Already"

The typical pattern of **jiù** is "Subject + time word + **jiù** + verb phrase + **le**" and it indicates that the time is earlier than expected, or that time has passed so fast that it's already time for the event to occur. Compare:

Wǒ míngtiān huí Měiguó.	I am going back to US tomorrow. (general).
Wǒ míngtiān jiù huí Měiguóle.	I am going back to US tomorrow. (**Míngtiān** is earlier than expected).
Tā zuótiān wǎnshàng liùdiǎn chīfàn.	He/She ate at 6 pm last night. (general)
Tā zuótiān wǎnshàng liùdiǎn jiù chīfànle.	It was only 6pm yesterday evening, but she/he had already had dinner.
Wǒmen zuótiān qìngzhù Lǐ Yángde shēngrì.	We celebrated Li Yang's birthday yesterday. (general statement)
Wǒmen zuótiān jiù qìngzhù Lǐ Yángde shēngrìle.	We already celebrated Li Yang's birthday yesterday.

GRAMMAR NOTE   Using the Adverb **Gāng** to Mean "Just"

Gāng is an adverb meaning "just, just now." It needs to be placed between the subject and the verb phrase. The event or the verb **gāng** refers to can be recent or long ago. Examples:

Tā gāng lái.	He/She just came.
Lǐ Yáng gāng zǒu.	Li Yang just left.
Wǒ gāng gěi nǐ dǎ diànhuà.	I just called you.
Wǒ qùnián gāng lái, míngtiān jiù yào zǒule.	I just came last year, and I am leaving tomorrow.

GRAMMAR NOTE

Using the Pattern "Subject + Verb + **le** + Quantified noun" to Express Completion

You have learned "Verb + **le**" to indicate completion of the verb in Lesson 13, such as **Nǐ kànle yīsheng ma** ("Did you see a doctor?"). Verb + **le** is often followed by a quantified noun. Examples:

Wǒ yàole yíliàng chūzūqìchē.	I reserved a taxi.
Wáng Mǐn mǎile yíjiàn yīfu.	Wang Min bought a shirt/dress.
Gāo Zhì'ān zhè yīnián xuéle hěn duō.	Gao Zhi'an has learned a lot this year.
Yīsheng gěi wǒ kāile yìxiē yào.	The doctor prescribed some medicine for me.

CULTURAL NOTE   Receiving a Compliment

When receiving a compliment such as **Nǐde Zhōngwén hěn hǎo** ("Your Chinese is good"), Chinese people tend to remain humble instead of accepting it. Instead of accepting the compliment by saying **xièxie** or **duōxiè**. Instead, you can say **náli** to mean "don't mention it" or "you are too kind" to show your humbleness. You have learned **náli** as a response to **xièxie** in Lesson 11. **Náli** is also a humble response to a compliment.

Pattern Practice 1

Practice saying the following phrases.
Subject 1 + **qǐng** + Subject 2 + verb phrase

Xièxie nǐ qǐng wǒ chīfàn.	Thank you for inviting me to dinner.
Xièxie nǐ qǐng wǒ chàng KTV.	Thank you for inviting me to karaoke.
Wǒ qǐng nǐ kàn diànyǐng.	Let's go see a movie. My treat.
Nǐ míngtiān yǒu-méiyou shíjiān?	Do you have time tomorrow?
Wǒ qǐng nǐ hē kāfēi.	Let's have coffee. My treat.

Pattern Practice 2

Practice saying the following phrases.
Subject + **zhēn** + stative verb

Zhōngwén zhēn yǒuyìsi.	(The) Chinese (language) is really interesting.
Zhèrde yīfu zhēn guì.	The clothes here are really expensive.
Diànzǐ yóujiàn zhēn fāngbiàn.	Email is really convenient.
Táiwān cài zhēn hǎochī.	Taiwanese cuisine is really tasty.
Bōshìdùnde dōngtiān zhēn lěng.	The winter in Boston is really cold.

Pattern Practice 3

Subject + time word + **jiù** + verb phrase + **le**

Zhāng Lǎoshī jīntiān shàngwǔ qīdiǎn jiù láile.	Professor Zhang came as early as 7 am this morning. (Prof. Zhang doesn't usually come so early.)
Túshūguǎn jīntiān liùdiǎn jiù kāile.	The library is open as early as 6 am today. (It is not usually open so early.)
Gāo Zhì'ān míngtiān jiù yào huí Měiguóle.	Gao Zhi'an is already going back to US tomorrow. (Time has passed so quickly that it's already time for Gao Zhi'an to return home).
Wǒ jīntiān sāndiǎn jiù qù yùndòngle.	I went to exercise at 3 pm today. (I don't usually exercise so early.)

Pattern Practice 4

Subject + **gāng** + verb phrase

Wǒ gāng lái.	I just came.
Wǒ gāng chīle yào.	I just took medicine.
Wǒ gāng qù mǎile yìdiǎnr dōngxi.	I just went to buy a few things.
Wáng Mín gāng zǒu.	Wang Min just left.
Gāo Zhì'ān gāng gěi Lǐ Yáng dǎle diànhuà.	Gao Zhi'an just called Li Yang.

Pattern Practice 5

Subject + verb + **le** + quantified noun

Wǒ zuótiān mǎile yíjiàn yīfu.	I bought a shirt/dress yesterday.
Wǒ gāng yàole yíliàng chūzūqìchē.	I just reserved a taxi.
Yīsheng gěi wǒ kāile yìxiē yào.	The doctor prescribed some medicine for me.
Lín Jīnglǐ hēle yìdiǎnr jiǔ.	Manager Lin had some wine.

Wǒ gāng gěi wǒ māma xiěle yíge   I just wrote an email to my mother.
diànzǐ yóujiàn.

EXERCISE 1

Fill in each blank with one of the following expressions.

qǐng	jiù	sòng	jìde

1. **Míngtiān shì nǐde shēngrì, wǒ _____ nǐ chīfàn, zěnmeyàng?**

2. **Wǒ _____ Lín Jīnglǐ yǒu liǎngge háizi, bú shì yīge.**

3. **Wǒ píngcháng liùdiǎn chīfàn, jīntiān wǔdiǎn _____ chīfànle.**

4. A: **Wǒ míngtiān _____ nǐ qù jīchǎng.**
   B: **Xièxie.**

EXERCISE 2

Answer each of the following questions in Chinese.

1. **Nǐ chángcháng qǐng péngyǒu chīfàn ma?**
2. **Nǐ chángcháng xiě diànzǐ yóujiàn ma?**
3. **Nǐde Zhōngwén yuèláiyuè hǎole ma?**
4. **Nǐ juéde shíjiān kuài-búkuài?**

EXERCISE 3

Translate the following dialogues into Chinese.

1. A: Thank you for inviting me to dinner tonight.
   B: You are welcome. Happy Birthday!
   A: Thank you.

2. A: Time passes so fast. You are going back to the US tomorrow.
   B: Yes. I remember I just came in June last year, and I am leaving tomorrow.
   A: Let us keep in touch via email.
   B: Absolutely.

3. A: Do you need a ride to the airport?
   B: No, thank you. I have reserved a taxi.
   A: When are you leaving tomorrow?
   B: 10 am.

EXERCISE 4

Read the following passage and answer the questions in English.

Lǐ Yáng,

Wǒ huí dào (returned to) **Bōshìdùn le. Wǒde bàba māma hěn gāoxìng** (happy). **Wǒde Zhōngwén lǎoshī yě shuō wǒde Zhōngwén yuèláiyuè hǎole. Xièxie nǐ zhè yīniánde bāngzhù** (help), **wǒ xuéle hěn duō.**

Bǎochí liánluò,
Gāo Zhì'ān

---

1. Who writes this email? Who is the recipient?

   _____

2. Where is the sender now?

   _____

3. What does the sender's Chinese teacher think about his/her Chinese?

   _____

4. What does the sender think about his/her past year in China?

   _____

5. If you were the recipient, how would you respond to the ending "**Bǎochí liánluò**"?

   _____

Airport signs in Simplified Chinese

Airport signs in Traditional Chinese

Newspapers in Simplified Chinese

LESSON 20

Introduction to
the Chinese Writing System (II)

In Lesson 10, you have learned the brief history of Chinese characters and their six ways of formation. In this lesson, we will introduce the correlation between traditional characters and simplified characters and follow these with another set of 25 common characters.

Traditional Characters vs. Simplified Characters

The history of simplification of Chinese characters has been a long one. As mentioned in Lesson 10, Chinese characters have gone through a few significant evolutions in forms from **Jiǎgǔwén** (oracle bone inscriptions) to **Kǎishū** (regular script), and those significant evolutions for the most part involved simplification in forms or strokes. For instance, the key difference between **Kǎishū** (regular script) and its predecessor **Lìshū** (Clerical script) is that **Kǎishū** are thinner and simpler in strokes. Compare the character **jù** 懼 (to fear) in both scripts:

Lìshū	Kǎishū
懼	懼

Two forms of Chinese characters are in use in contemporary Chinese-speaking societies: Mainland China has adopted simplified characters (**Jiǎntǐzì**) while Taiwan and Hong Kong use traditional characters (**Fántǐzì**). Traditional characters inherit the long history of Chinese writing system and do not contain the newly created simplified characters promulgated and standardized by the Chinese government since the 1950s in an effort to increase literacy. The character simplification movements by the Chinese government in the 1950s and 1960s have affected a significant number of traditional characters, but the majority of novice-level characters remain intact. Take a look at the 25 characters introduced in Lesson 10:

Traditional Character	Simplified Character	Pinyin	English
一	一	yī	one
二	二	èr	two
三	三	sān	three
四	四	sì	four

Traditional Character	Simplified Character	Pinyin	English
五	五	**wǔ**	five
六	六	**liù**	six
七	七	**qī**	seven
八	八	**bā**	eight
九	九	**jiǔ**	nine
十	十	**shí**	ten
百	百	**bǎi**	hundred
千	千	**qiān**	thousand
元	元	**yuán**	dollar
你	你	**nǐ**	you
我	我	**wǒ**	I, me
他	他	**tā**	he, him
她	她	**tā**	she, her
是	是	**shì**	be
謝	谢	**xiè**	thank
中	中	**zhōng**	middle
美	美	**měi**	pretty, beautiful
國	国	**guó**	nation, country
人	人	**rén**	people
歲	岁	**suì**	years of age
好	好	**hǎo**	good

Among these 25 characters, only 3 are simplified: 謝 = 谢, 國 = 国, and 歲 = 岁. These simplifications come with rules. For instance, 謝 is simplified by replacing its left semantic component 言 with 讠, which resembles its cursive form in calligraphy. If you are interested in knowing more about these rules, you can refer to *Learning Mandarin Chinese Characters Volume 1 & Volume 2* by Tuttle for details.

Since the simplified characters did not gain official recognition until the 1950s in Mainland China, most original signs of historical sites, famous restaurants, and leading newspapers were still written in traditional characters. In Hong Kong and Taiwan, due to the increasing interactions with Mainland China or simply for the sake of saving time, you will also encounter simplified characters. As learners of Chinese, you should aim to be able to read both versions of characters but choose one version in writing, as most Chinese intellectuals do.

25 More Characters

Traditional Character	Simplified Character	Pinyin	English	Compounds
先生	先生	xiān / shēng	first / student, be born	先生 **Xiānsheng** (Mr.) 生 loses its tone in the compound 先生.
小姐	小姐	xiǎo / jiě	small, little / sister (older)	小姐 **Xiǎojie** (Ms) 姐 loses its tone in the compound 小姐.
王	王	Wáng	Wang (surname)	王先生 **Wáng Xiānsheng** (Mr. Wang)
李	李	Lǐ	Li (surname)	李小姐 **Lǐ Xiǎojie** (Ms Li)
請問	请问	qǐng / wèn	please / ask	請問/请问 **Qǐng wèn** (Excuse me; may I ask)
去	去	qù	go	
什麼	什么	shén / me		什麼／什么 **shénme** (what)
哪	哪	nǎ	where	
這	这	zhè	this	
那	那	nà	that	
叫	叫	jiào	be called	
不	不	bù/bú	not (negation word)	不是 **bú shì** (not be)
呢	呢	ne	what about	您呢? **Nín ne?** (What about you?)
嗎	吗	ma	(sentence-final question word)	
您	您	nín	you (polite form)	
英	英	yīng	British, brave	英文 **Yīngwén** (English language)
文	文	wén	language	中文 **Zhōngwén** (Chinese language)

Traditional Character	Simplified Character	Pinyin	English	Compounds
北	北	**běi**	north	
京	京	**jīng**	capital	北京 **Běijīng** (Beijing)
會	会	**huì**	can (indicates capability)	會不會 / 会不会 **huì-búhuì** (Can or cannot?)
說	说	**shuō**	speak	

EXERCISE

Based on the English translation, find the correct word to be put into the blanks.

去	京	吗	你	不
说	您	请	中	那

1. 王先生，＿＿＿＿＿＿ 好。(polite)
   Hi, Mr. Wang.

2. 李小姐，＿＿＿＿＿＿ 好。(general)
   Hi, Ms Li.

3. 王先生，你 ＿＿＿＿＿＿ 哪？
   Mr. Wang, where are you going?

4. ＿＿＿＿＿＿ 问，这是什么？
   Excuse me, what is this?

5. ＿＿＿＿＿＿ 是什么？
   What is that?

6. 那是"六"＿＿＿＿＿＿？
   Is that "six"?

7. 我会 ＿＿＿＿＿＿ 英文。
   I speak English.

8. 你会说 ＿＿＿＿＿＿ 文吗？
   Do you speak Chinese?

9. 我 _____ 会说英文，你呢？
   I don't speak English. How about you?

10. 李先生不去北 _____ 吗？
    Isn't Mr. Li going to Beijing?

Note

As mentioned in Lesson 1, characters in a sentence do not have space in between, such as 我是美国人 ("I am American"). You can use a comma (,) to separate sentences and end a sentence with a small circle (。) or a question mark (?) depending on the nature of the sentence.

The Bund is well known in Shanghai.

The Great Wall of China is a much visited tourist spot.

English-Pinyin Glossary

A

a little yīdiǎn(r)
a lot hěn duō
about (adv) chàbuduō
accent kǒuyīn
activity huódòng
acupuncture zhēnjiǔ
address dìzhǐ
afterward hòulái
again zài; yòu
age niánjì
ago yǐqián
agree tóngyì
air conditioner kōngtiáo
airlines hángkōng gōngsī
airplane; flight fēijī
airport jīchǎng
alcohol jiǔ
allergy guòmǐn
already yǐjīng
also yě
although suīrán
always zǒngshì
and hé; gēn
angry shēngqì
animal dòngwù
antibiotic kàngshēngsù
antiques gǔdǒng
apartment gōngyù
apologize dàoqiàn
appetizer qiáncài
apple píngguǒ
approximately dàgài
architecture jiànzhù
arrival time dàodá shíjiān
art yìshù
ask wèn
ATM tíkuǎnjī
authentic dìdào
autumn qiūtiān

B

baby yīng'ér
backpack bēibāo
bad huài
baggage, luggage xínglǐ
bakery hōngpéidiàn
banana xiāngjiāo
bandage bēngdài
bank yínháng
bar jiǔbā
barbershop lǐfàdiàn
bargain (v) shājià
baseball bàngqiú
basketball lánqiú
bathroom wèishēngjiān
battery diànchí
be shì
be at, be located at zài
beach hǎitān
beautiful, pretty piàoliang
beauty salon měiróngdiàn
because yīnwèi
bed chuáng
bedroom wòshì
beef niúròu
beer píjiǔ
beverage yǐnliào
Bible shèngjīng
big dà
birthday shēngrì
bitter kǔ
black hēisè
blow-dryer chuīfēngjī
blue lánsè
book shū
boring méiyǒu yìsi
bowl wǎn
boy nánhái
boyfriend nánpéngyǒu
bread miànbāo
breakfast zǎofàn
brown zōngsè
Buddha fó
bus gōngchē
busy máng
butter niúyóu
buy mǎi

C

cab, taxi **chūzū qìchē**
café **kāfēi diàn**
can (*auxiliary v*) **néng; kěyǐ**
car **chē**
careful **xiǎoxīn**
cash **xiànjīn**
cell phone **shǒujī**
champagne **xiāngbīn**
cheap **piányi**
check (in a restaurant) **mǎidān**
cheese **qǐsī**
chicken **jīròu**
chili pepper/chili **làjiāo**
chocolate **qiǎokèlì**
chopstick **kuàizi**
Christmas **Shèngdànjié**
church **jiàotáng**
cigarette **yān**
classmate **tóngxué**
clean (*adj*) **gānjìng**
clever **cōngming**
close (*adj*) **jìn**
closed (shops) **guānmén**
clothes **yīfu**
coffee **kāfēi**
cold (*adj*) **lěng**
college, university **dàxué**
color (*n*) **yánsè**
comfortable **shūfu**
company **gōngsī**
computer **diànnǎo**
convenient **fāngbiàn**
cool **kù**
correct (*adj*) **duì**
credit card **xìnyòngkǎ**
culture **wénhuà**
cup (*n*) **bēi**

D

dance club **bèngdī**
dangerous **wēixiǎn**
daughter **nǚ'ér**
day **tiān**
debit card **tíkuǎnkǎ**
delicious **hǎo chī**

departure time **chūfā shíjiān**
dessert **tiánshí**
diarrhea **fùxiè**
dictionary **zìdiǎn**
different **bùtóng**
difficult **nán**
dinner **wǎnfàn**
dirty **zāng**
discount **dǎzhé**
dish (of food) **cài**
dizziness **tóuyūn**
doctor **yīshēng**
dog **gǒu**
dollar **yuán**
drink (*v*) **hē**
dry **gān**

E

east **dōng**
easy **jiǎndān**
eat **chī**
egg **dàn**
email **diànzǐ yóujiàn**
embassy **dàshǐguǎn**
emergency **jǐnjí shìqing**
entrance **rùkǒu**
evening **bāngwǎn**
every day **měitiān**
everyone **měige rén**
exchange (money) **huàn**
excuse me **qǐng wèn**
exit (*n*) **chūkǒu**
expensive **guì**
eye **yǎnjīng**

F

fake (*adj*) **jiǎde**
family **jiārén**
famous **yǒumíng**
far **yuǎn**
father **bàba**
fax (*n*) **chuánzhēn**
fee **fèiyòng**
fever **fāshāo**
fish (*n*) **yú**
fit (right size) **héshì**

flower **huā**
food **shíwù**
foreigner **wàiguórén**
forget **wàng**
fork (*n*) **chāzi**
fragrant **xiāng**
frequently **jīngcháng**
fresh **xīnxiān**
friend **péngyǒu**
fruit **shuǐguǒ**
funny **hǎoxiào**

G
garlic **suàn**
gas **yóu**
gas station **jiāyóuzhàn**
gift **lǐwù**
ginger **jiāng**
girlfriend **nǚpéngyǒu**
go **qù**
go home **huíjiā**
goodbye **zàijiàn**
gray **huīsè**
green (color) **lǜsè**
guide (person) **dǎoyóu**
gym **jiànshēnfáng**

H
habit **xíguàn**
handsome **shuài**
happy **kuàilè**
hat **màozi**
have **yǒu**
have to **děi**
headache **tóuténg**
hear **tīng**
heart attack **xīnzàngbìng**
heat stroke **zhòngshǔ**
heavy **zhòng**
hello **nǐ hǎo**
hello (answering the phone) **wéi**
help (*v*) **bāng**
here **zhèr**
high **gāo**
history **lìshǐ**
home **jiā**

hope **xīwàng**
hospitable **yǒushàn**
hospital **yīyuàn**
hot **rè**
hot tea **rè chá**
hot water **rè shuǐ**
hotel **lǚguǎn**
hour **xiǎoshí**
how far? **duōyuǎn**
how long? **duōcháng shíjiān**
how much (money)? **duōshǎo qián**
how old? **duōdà**
humid **cháoshī**
hungry **è**
hurry up **gǎnkuài**
husband **xiānsheng**

I
ice cream **bīngjīlín**
iced tea **bīng chá**
iced water **bīng shuǐ**
if **rúguǒ; yàoshi**
immediately **mǎshàng**
important **zhòngyào**
information center **xúnwèn zhōngxīn**
interesting **yǒu yìsī**
international **guójì**
Internet **wǎngluò**
Internet Cafe **wǎngbā**
invite **yāoqǐng**
itchy **yǎng**

J
jacket **wàitào**
job **gōngzuò**
juice **guǒzhī**

K
karaoke **chàng KTV**
key **yàoshi**
know **zhīdào**

L
ladies' room **nǚ wèishēngjiān**
lake **hú**
lamb (meat) **yángròu**

language yǔyán
large dà
last month shàngge yuè
last week shàngge xīngqi
last year qùnián
late wǎn
learn xué
left (n) zuǒbiān
library túshūguǎn
like (v) xǐhuan
listen tīng
live (v) (reside in) zhù
long cháng
look (v) kàn
look for zhǎo
lunch zhōngfàn

M

mail xìn
make a phone call dǎ diànhuà
make-up huàzhuāng
man nánrén
manager jīnglǐ
mango mángguǒ
map dìtú
market shìchǎng
maybe yěxǔ
meat ròu
medicine yào
meditate jìngzuò
men's room nán wèishēngjiān
menu càidān
milk niúnǎi
minute (time) fēn
money qián
month yuè
more (-er) bǐjiào
morning zǎoshàng
mosquito wénzi
mosquito repellent qūwénjì
most (-est) zuì
mother māma
motorbike mótuōchē
mountain shān
movie diànyǐng

movie theater diànyǐngyuàn
mung bean dòuyácài
museum bówùguǎn
mushroom xiānggū
music yīnyuè
must (aux. v) děi

N

name (n) míngzi
nation guójiā
nausea zuò'ǒu
near (adj) kàojìn
necessary bìyào
need (v) xūyào
nervous jǐnzhāng
never cóngbù
new xīn
New Taiwan Dollars (Taiwan currency)
  Xīntáibì
news xīnwén
newspaper bàozhǐ
next month xiàge yuè
next week xiàge xīngqī
next year míngnián
night wǎnshàng
nightclub jiǔbā
noisy chǎo
north běi
not yet hái méi
now xiànzài

O

often chángcháng
okay hǎo
old (used) jiù
older brother gēge
older sister jiějie
on the left-hand side zuǒshǒubiān
on the right-hand side yòushǒubiān
only zhǐ
open (v) kāi
opinion yìjiàn
opportunity jīhuì
or (A or B?) háishì
or (A or B...) huòshì
orange (color) chéngsè

orange (fruit) **chéngzi**
orange juice **chéngzhī**
order (*v*) (for food) **diǎn**
over there **nàr**

P

pain (*n*) **téngtòng**
painkiller **zhǐténgyào**
painting (painted picture) **huà**
pair of chopsticks **yīshuāng kuàizi**
pair of shoes **yīshuāng xié**
panda **xióngmāo**
pants **kùzi**
papaya **mùguā**
paper napkin **cānjīnzhǐ**
park **gōngyuán**
parking lot **tíngchēchǎng**
passport **hùzhào**
patient (*n*) **bìngrén**
patient (*adj*) **nàixīn**
pay (*v*) **fù**
peach **táo**
peanut **huāshēng**
pear **lí**
pen **bǐ**
pencil **qiānbǐ**
pepper **hújiāo**
perfume **xiāngshuǐ**
person, people **rén**
pharmacy **yàodiàn**
phone **diànhuà**
phone number **diànhuà hàomǎ**
photo, picture **zhàopiān**
pick up (a car, an item) **qǔ**
pick up (a friend) **jiē**
pineapple **bōluó**
pink (color) **fěnsè**
plane ticket **jīpiào**
police **jǐngchá**
polite **kèqi**
pomelo **yòuzi**
popular **shòuhuānyíng**
pork **zhūròu**
possible **kěnéng**
post office **yóujú**
postcard **míngxìnpiān**

potato **tǔdòu**
practice **liànxí**
prepare **zhǔnbèi**
price (*n*) **jiàqián**
professor **jiàoshòu**
project (*n*) **jìhuà**
promise (*v*) **dāyìng**
pronounce **fāyīn**
public phone **gōngyòng diànhuà**
purple (color) **zǐsè**
purse **qiánbāo**

Q

quality **zhìliàng**
quantity **shùliàng**
question, problem **wèntí**
quick **kuài**
quiet (place) **ānjìng**

R

rain (*v*) **xiàyǔ**
rambutan **hóngmáodān**
rarely **hěn shǎo**
reason (*n*) **lǐyóu**
receipt **shōujù**
red (color) **hóngsè**
red wine **hóngjiǔ**
refund (*v*) **tuìqián**
relationship **guānxi**
religion **zōngjiào**
rent (*v*) **zū**
repeat (say again) **zài shuō yībiàn**
restaurant **cāntīng**
restroom **xǐshǒujiān**
return **huán**
rice (cooked) **mǐfàn**
right (*adj*) **duì**
river **hé**
room **fángjiān**
run (*v*) **pǎo**

S

sad **nánguò**
safe (*adj*) **ānquán**
salad **shālācài**
salt **yán**

salty **xián**
say (*v*) **shuō**
school **xuéxiào**
sea **hǎi**
seafood **hǎixiān**
season (*n*) **jìjié**
see **kàn**
sell **mài**
send **jì**
shampoo **xǐfashuǐ**
shirt **chènyī**
shoes **xié**
shop (*n*) **shāngdiàn**
shopping mall **gòuwù zhōngxīn**
short (in length) **duǎn**
shorts **duǎnkù**
sick **shēngbìng**
sit **zuò**
size **dàxiǎo**
skirt **qúnzi**
sleep (*v*) **shuì**
sleeping pills **ānmiányào**
sleepy **kùn**
slow(ly) **màn**
small **xiǎo**
snack (*n*) **diǎnxīn**
snow (*v*) **xiàxuě**
soap (*n*) **xiāngzào**
soccer **zúqiú**
sock (*n*) **wàzi**
soda (soft drink) **qìshuǐ**
sometimes **yǒude shíhou**
son **érzi**
sore throat **hóulóngténg**
soup **tāng**
south **nán**
souvenir **jìniànpǐn**
soy sauce **jiàngyóu**
speak **shuō**
special **tèbié**
spend **huā**
spicy **là**
spoon **sháozi**
sport (*n*) **yùndòng**
spring (season) **chūntiān**
stamp (*n*) **yóupiào**

stomach ache **wèiténg**
street **jiē**
study (learn) **xuéxí**
sugar **táng**
suggest **jiànyì**
summer **xiàtiān**
sunny **qíngtiān**
supermarket **chāoshì**
sweater **máoyī**
sweet (*adj*) **tián**
swim (*v*) **yóuyǒng**
swimming pool **yóuyǒngchí**

T

T-shirt **tīxùshān**
table **zhuōzi**
take pictures **zhàoxiàng**
talk (*v*) **shuōhuà**
tall **gāo**
tea **chá**
teacher **lǎoshī**
telephone **diànhuà**
television **diànshì**
temple **miào**
thank **xièxie**
think **xiǎng**
thirsty **kě**
this month **zhèige yuè**
this week **zhège xīngqi**
this year **jīnnián**
ticket **piào**
tight (fit) **jǐn**
time (*n*) **shíjiān**
tip (*n*) **xiǎofèi**
tired **lèi**
today **jīntiān**
toilet paper **wèishēngzhǐ**
tomato **xīhóngshì**
tomorrow **míngtiān**
tonight **jīnwǎn**
toothache **yáténg**
town **chéng**
traffic **jiāotōng**
train (*n*) **huǒchē**
train station **huǒchē zhàn**
translator (interpreter) **fānyì rényuán**

travel agency **lǔxíngshè**
try on (clothes, shoes) **shìchuān**
turkey **huǒjī**

U

umbrella **sǎn**
uncomfortable **bù shūfu**
understand **dǒng**
underwear **nèiyīkù**
urgent **jǐnjí**
US dollars **Měiyuán**
USA **Měiguó**
use (*v*) **yòng**
useful **yǒuyòng**
usually **tōngcháng**

V

vegetable **shūcài**
vegetarian dish **sùcài**
very **hěn**
vinegar **cù**
visit (*v*) **cānguān**

W

wait (*v*) **děng**
waiter **fúwùyuán**
walk (*v*) **zǒu**
want (*v*) **xiǎng; yào**
warm **nuǎn**
wash (hair, hands, clothes) **xǐ**
watch (*v*) **kàn**
water (*n*) **shuǐ**
watermelon **xīgua**

we (exclusive) **wǒmen**
we (inclusive) **zánmen**
wear (clothes, shoes) **chuān**
wear (hats) **dài**
weather **tiānqi**
week **xīngqī**
weekend **zhōumò**
welcome **huānyíng**
west **xī**
white **báisè**
white wine **báijiǔ**
wife **tàitai**
window seat **kàochuāng**
wine **jiǔ**
winter **dōngtiān**
withdraw money **qǔ qián**
woman **nǚrén**
word **zì; cí**
work (*v*)(*n*) **gōngzuò; zuògōng**
wrong **cuò**

Y

year **nián**
yellow **huángsè**
yesterday **zuótiān**
yogurt **suānnǎi**
younger brother **dìdi**
younger sister **mèimei**
yuan (Chinese currency) **yuán**

Z

zebra **bānmǎ**
zoo **dòngwùyuán**

Pinyin-English Glossary

A

ānjìng quiet (place)
ānmiányào sleeping pills
ānquán safe (*adj*)

B

bàba father
báijiǔ white wine
báisè white
bāng help (*v*)
bàngqiú baseball
bāngwǎn evening
bàozhǐ newspaper
běi north
bēi cup (*n*)
bēibāo backpack
bēngdài bandage
bèngdī dance club
bǐ pen
bǐjiào more (-*er*)
bīng chá iced tea
bīng shuǐ iced water
bīngjīlín ice cream
bìngrén patient (*n*)
bìyào necessary
bōluó pineapple
bówùguǎn museum
bù shūfu uncomfortable
bùtóng different

C

cài dish (of food)
càidān menu
cānguān visit (*v*)
cānjīnzhǐ paper napkin
cāntīng restaurant
chá tea
chàbuduō about (*adv*)
cháng long
chàng KTV karaoke (lit., sing karaoke)
chángcháng often
chǎo noisy
cháoshī humid
cháoshì supermarket

chāzi fork (*n*)
chē car
chéng town
chéngsè orange (color)
chéngzhī orange juice
chéngzi orange (fruit)
chènyī shirt
chī eat
chuān wear (clothes, shoes)
chuáng bed
chuánzhēn fax (*n*)
chūfā shíjiān departure time
chuīfēngjī blow-dryer
chūkǒu exit (*n*)
chūntiān spring (season)
chūzū qìchē cab, taxi
cóngbù never
cōngming clever
cù vinegar
cuò wrong

D

dà big, large
dǎ diànhuà make a phone call
dàgài approximately
dài wear (hats)
dàn egg
dàodá shíjiān arrival time
dàoqiàn apologize
dǎoyóu guide (person)
dàshǐguǎn embassy
dàxiǎo size
dàxué college, university
dāyìng promise (*v*)
dǎzhé discount
děi have to, must (*aux. v*)
děng wait (*v*)
diǎn order (*v*) (for food)
diànchí battery
diànhuà phone, telephone
diànhuà hàomǎ phone number
diànnǎo computer
diànshì television
diǎnxīn snack (*n*)

diànyǐng movie
diànyǐngyuàn movie theater
diànzǐ yóujiàn electronic mail, email
dìdào authentic
dìdi younger brother
dìtú map
dìzhǐ address
dǒng understand
dōng east
dōngtiān winter
dòngwù animal
dòngwùyuán zoo
dòuyácài mung bean
duǎn short (in length)
duǎnkù shorts
duì correct, right (*adj*)
duōcháng shíjiān how long?
duōdà how old?
duōshǎo qián how much (money)?
duōyuǎn how far?

E
è hungry
érzi son

F
fāngbiàn convenient
fángjiān room
fānyì rényuán translator (interpreter)
fāshāo fever
fāyīn pronounce
fēijī airplane; flight
fèiyòng fee
fēn minute (time)
fěnsè pink (color)
fó Buddha
fù pay (*v*)
fúwùyuán waiter
fùxiè diarrhea

G
gān dry
gānjìng clean (*adj*)
gǎnkuài hurry up
gāo high, tall
gēge older brother

gōngchē bus
gōngsī company
gōngyòng diànhuà public phone
gōngyù apartment
gōngyuán park
gōngzuò job, work (*v*) (*n*)
gǒu dog
gòuwù zhōngxīn shopping mall
guānmén closed (shops)
guānxi relationship
gǔdǒng antiques
guì expensive
guójì international
guójiā nation, country
guòmǐn allergy
guǒzhī juice

H
hǎi sea
hái méi not yet
háishì or (A or B?)
hǎitān beach
hǎixiān seafood
hángkōng gōngsī airline
hǎo okay, good
hǎo chī delicious
hǎoxiào funny
hē drink (*v*)
hé river
hé, gēn and
hēisè black
hěn very
hěn duō a lot
hěn shǎo rarely
héshì fit (right size)
hóngjiǔ red wine
hóngmáodān rambutan
hōngpéidiàn bakery
hóngsè red (color)
hòulái afterward
hóulóngténg sore throat
hú lake
huā flower, spend
huà to paint, painting (painted picture)
huài bad
huàn exchange (money)

huán return
huángsè yellow
huānyíng welcome
huāshēng peanut
huàzhuāng make-up
huíjiā go home
huīsè gray
hújiāo pepper
huǒchē train (n)
huǒchē zhàn train station
huódòng activity
huǒjī turkey
huòshì or (A or B...)
hùzhào passport

J

jì send
jiā home
jiǎde fake (adj)
jiǎndān easy
jiāng ginger
jiàngyóu soy sauce
jiànshēnfáng gymnasium, gym
jiànyì suggest
jiànzhù architecture
jiàoshòu professor
jiàotáng church
jiāotōng traffic
jiàqián price (n)
jiārén family
jiāyóuzhàn gas station
jīchǎng airport
jiē pick up (a friend)
jiē street
jiějie older sister
jìhuà project (n)
jīhuì opportunity
jìjié season (n)
jìn close (adj)
jǐn tight (fit)
jǐngchá police
jīngcháng frequently
jīnglǐ manager
jìngzuò meditate
jìniànpǐn souvenir
jǐnjí urgent

jǐnjí shìqíng emergency
jīnnián this year
jīntiān today
jīnwǎn tonight
jǐnzhāng nervous
jīpiào plane ticket
jīròu chicken (meat)
jiù old (used)
jiǔ alcohol, wine
jiǔbā bar, nightclub

K

kāfēi coffee
kāfēi diàn café
kāi open (v)
kàn look (v), see, watch (v)
kàngshēngsù antibiotic
kàochuāng window seat
kàojìn near (adj)
kě thirsty
kěnéng possible
kèqi polite
kōngtiáo air conditioner
kǒuyīn accent
kù cool
kǔ bitter
kuài quick
kuàilè happy
kuàizi chopsticks
kùn sleepy
kùzi pants

L

là spicy
làjiāo chili pepper, chili
lánqiú basketball
lánsè blue
lǎoshī teacher
lèi tired
lěng cold (adj)
lí pear
liànxí practice
lǐfàdiàn barbershop
lìshǐ history
lǐwù gift
lǐyóu reason (n)

lǚguǎn hotel
lǜsè green (color)
lǚxíngshè travel agency

M

mài sell
mǎi buy
mǎidān check (in a restaurant)
māma mother
màn slow(ly)
máng busy
mángguǒ mango
máoyī sweater
màozi hat
mǎshàng immediately
měige rén everyone
Měiguó USA
mèimei younger sister
měiróngdiàn beauty salon
měitiān every day
méiyǒu yìsi boring
Měiyuán US dollars
miànbāo bread
miào temple
mǐfàn rice (cooked)
míngnián next year
míngtiān tomorrow
míngxìnpiàn postcard
míngzi name (*n*)
mótuōchē motorbike
mùguā papaya

N

nàixīn patient (*adj*)
nán difficult
nán south
nán wèishēngjiān men's room
nánguò sad
nánhái boy
nánpéngyǒu boyfriend
nánrén man
nàr over there
nèiyīkù underwear
néng; kéyǐ can (*aux v*)
nǐ hǎo hello
nián year
niánjì age

niúnǎi milk
niúròu beef
niúyóu butter
nuǎn warm
nǚ wèishēngjiān ladies' room
nǚ'ér daughter
nǚpéngyǒu girlfriend
nǚrén woman

P

pǎo run (*v*)
péngyǒu friend
piányi cheap
piào ticket
piàoliang beautiful, pretty
píjiǔ beer
píngguǒ apple

Q

qián money
qiánbāo purse, wallet
qiānbǐ pen
qiáncài appetizer
qiǎokèlì chocolate
qǐng wèn excuse me
qíngtiān sunny
qìshuǐ soda (soft drink)
qǐsī cheese
qiūtiān autumn
qù go
qǔ pick up (a car, an item)
qǔ qián withdraw money
qùnián last year
qúnzi skirt
qūwénjì mosquito repellent

R

rè hot
rè chá hot tea
rè shuǐ hot water
rén person, people
ròu meat
rúguǒ; yàoshi if
rùkǒu entrance

S

săn umbrella
shājià bargain
shālācài salad
shān mountain
shāngdiàn shop (n)
shàngge xīngqi last week
shàngge yuè last month
sháozi spoon
shēngbing sick
Shèngdànjié Christmas
shèngjīng Bible
shēngqì angry
shēngrì birthday
shì be
shícháng often
shìcháng market
shìchuān try on (clothes, shoes)
shíjiān time (n)
shíwù food
shòuhuānyíng popular
shǒujī cell phone
shōujù receipt
shū book
shuài handsome
shūcài vegetable
shūfu comfortable
shuì sleep (v)
shuǐ water (n)
shuǐguǒ fruit
shùliàng quantity
shuō say (v), speak
shuōhuà talk (v)
suàn garlic
suān sour
suānnǎi yogurt
sùcài vegetarian dish
suīrán although

T

tàitai wife
táng sugar
tāng soup
táo peach
tèbié special
téngtòng pain (n)

tián sweet
tiān day, sky
tiānqi weather
tiánshí dessert
tíkuǎnjī ATM
tíkuǎnkǎ debit card
tīng hear, listen
tíngchēchǎng parking lot
tīxùshān T-shirt
tōngcháng usually
tóngxué classmate
tóngyì agree
tóuténg headache
tóuyūn dizziness
tǔdòu potato
tuìqián refund (v)
túshūguǎn library

W

wàiguórén foreigner
wàitào jacket
wǎn bowl
wǎn late
wǎnfàn dinner
wàng forget
wǎngbā Internet Café
wǎngluò Internet
wǎnshàng night
wàzi sock (n)
wéi hello (answering the telephone)
wèishēngjiān bathroom, toilet
wèishēngzhǐ toilet paper
wèiténg stomachache
wēixiǎn dangerous
wèn ask
wénhuà culture
wèntí question, problem
wénzi mosquito
wǒmen we (exclusive)
wòshì bedroom

X

xǐ wash (hair, hands, clothes)
xī west
xiàge xīngqī next week
xiàge yuè next month

xián salty
xiāng fragrant
xiǎng think
xiǎng; yào want (*v*)
xiāngbīn champagne
xiānggū mushroom
xiāngjiāo banana
xiāngshuǐ perfume
xiāngzào soap (*n*)
xiànjīn cash
xiānsheng husband
xiànzài now
xiǎo small
xiǎofèi tip (*n*)
xiǎoshí hour
xiǎoxīn careful
xiàtiān summer
xiàxuě snowing
xiàyǔ raining
xié shoes
xièxie thank
xǐfashuǐ shampoo
xīgua watermelon
xíguàn habit
xīhóngshì tomato
xǐhuan like (*v*)
xìn mail
xīn new
xínglǐ baggage, luggage
xīngqī week
Xīntáibì New Taiwan Dollars
  (Taiwan currency)
xīnwén news
xīnxiān fresh
xìnyòngkǎ credit card
xīnzàngbìng heart attack
xióngmāo panda
xǐshǒujiān restroom
xīwàng hope
xué learn
xuéxí study (learn)
xuéxiào school
xúnwèn zhōngxīn information center
xūyào need (*v*)

Y

yán salt
yān cigarette
yǎng itchy
yángròu lamb (meat)
yǎnjīng eye
yánsè color
yào medicine
yàodiàn pharmacy
yāoqǐng invite
yàoshi key
yáténg toothache
yě also
yěxǔ maybe
yīdiǎn(r) a little
yīfu clothes (*n*)
yìjiàn opinion
yǐjīng already
yīng'ér baby
yínháng bank
yǐnliào beverage
yīnwèi because
yīnyuè music
yǐqián ago, before
yīshēng doctor
yìshù art
yīshuāng kuàizi pair of chopsticks
yīshuāng xié pair of shoes
yīyuàn hospital
yòng use (*v*)
yóu gas
yǒu have
yǒu yìsī interesting
yǒude shíhou sometimes
yóujú post office
yǒumíng famous
yóupiào postal stamp
yǒushàn hospitable
yòushǒubiān on the right-hand side
yóuyǒng swim (*v*)
yǒuyòng useful
yóuyǒngchí swimming pool
yòuzi pomelo
yú fish (*n*)
yuán dollar, yuan (Chinese currency)
yuǎn far

yuè month
yùndòng sport (*n*)
yǔyán language

Z

zài be at, be located at
zài shuō yībiàn repeat (say again)
zài; yòu again
zàijiàn goodbye
zāng dirty
zánmen we (inclusive)
zǎofàn breakfast
zǎoshàng morning
zhǎo look for
zhàopiān photo, picture
zhàoxiàng take pictures
zhège xīngqi this week
zhèige yuè this month
zhēnjiǔ acupuncture
zhèr here
zhǐ only
zhīdào know, recognize
zhìliàng quality
zhǐténgyào painkiller
zhòng heavy

zhōngfàn lunch
zhòngshǔ heat stroke
zhòngyào important
zhōumò weekend
zhù live (*v*), reside
zhǔnbèi prepare
zhuōzi table
zhūròu pork
zì, cí word
zìdiǎn dictionary
zǐsè purple
zōngjiào religion
zōngsè brown (color)
zǒngshì always
zǒu walk (*v*)
zū rent (*v*)
zuì most (-*est*)
zuò sit
zuǒ'ǒu nausea
zuǒbiān left (*n*)
zuǒshǒubiān on the left-hand side
zuótiān yesterday
zúqiú soccer

Answer Key

LESSON 3
Exercise 1
1. nǐ hǎo
2. nǎr
3. ne
4. zàijiàn

Exercise 2
1. A: Èh, nǐ hǎo.
   B: Nǐ hǎo, nǐ qù nǎr?
   A: Wǒ qù shūdiàn, nǐ ne?
   B: Wǒ qù shítáng.

2. A: Èh, nǐ qù nǎr?
   B: Wǒ qù mǎi yìdiǎnr dōngxi, nǐ ne?
   A: Wǒ qù chīfàn.
   B: En, zàijiàn.
   A: Zàijiàn.

Exercise 3
You: Èh, Lǐ Ān, nǐ hǎo.
An: Nǐ hǎo.
You: Nǐ qù nǎr?
An: Wǒ qù shítáng, nǐ ne?
You: Wǒ qù mǎi yìdiǎnr dōngxi.
An: En, zàijiàn.
You: Zàijiàn.

LESSON 4
Exercise 1
1. jiào
2. shì
3. yě
4. ma

Exercise 2
1. Wǒ jiào (your name)
2. Wǒ shì (your country name) rén
3. Wǒ xué (your major)

Exercise 3
1. A: Nǐ hǎo, nǐ jiào shénme míngzi?
   B: Wǒ jiào Wáng Mǐn, nǐ ne?
   A: Wǒ jiào Lǐ Yáng.
2. A: Nǐ hǎo, nǐ shì něiguó rén?
   B: Wǒ shì Déguó rén, nǐ ne?
   A: Wǒ shì Rìběn rén. Nǐ xué shénme?
   B: Wǒ xué Zhōngwén.
   A: Wǒ yě xué Zhōngwén.

Exercise 4
You:	Nǐ hǎo, nǐ jiào shénme míngzi?
Your classmate:	Wǒ jiào (name), nǐ ne?
You:	Wǒ jiào (name). Nǐ shì něiguó rén?
Your classmate:	Wǒ shì (country name) rén.
You:	Nǐ xué shénme?
Your classmate:	Wǒ xué (major), nǐ ne?
You:	Wǒ xué (major).

LESSON 5
Exercise 1
1. nín hǎo
2. de
3. qǐng; ge
4. Bié kèqi

Exercise 2
1. A: Lǎoshī, nín hǎo, wǒ jiào Lǐ Lì, wǒ shì wùlǐxìde jiāohuàn xuésheng.
   B: Nǐ hǎo.

2. A: Lǎoshī, wǒ xiǎng qǐng wèn nín yíge wèntí.
   B: Hǎo, qǐng zuò.

3. A: Lǎoshī, xièxie.
   B: Bié kèqi, zàijiàn.
   A: Zàijiàn.

Exercise 3

You: Lǎoshī, nín hǎo, wǒ shì
         jīngjìxuéxìde jiāohuàn
         xuésheng, wǒ jiào ...
Teacher: Nǐ hǎo.
You: Wǒ xiǎng qǐng wèn nín yíge
         wèntí.
Teacher: Hǎo.
You: (ask the question)...

LESSON 6
Exercise 1
1. zěnmeyàng
2. Tǐng
3. yìqǐ
4. jǐ

Exercise 2
1. Wǒ ...
2. Xiànzài (number) diǎn.
3. Wǒ ...

Exercise 3
1. A: Èh, nǐ zěnmeyàng?
   B: Hái xíng, nǐ ne?
   A: Tǐng mángde.

2. A: Èh, míngtiān yìqǐ dǎ páiqiú
      zěnmeyàng?
   B: Hǎo, míngtiān jǐdiǎn?
   A: Xiàwǔ sāndiǎn.
   B: Hǎo, míngtiān jiàn.
   A: Míngtiān jiàn.

3. A: Nǐ jǐdiǎn qù chīfàn?
   B: Shí'èrdiǎn.
   A: Hǎo, wǒmen yìqǐ qù.
   B: Hǎo.

Exercise 4
A: Èh, míngtiān yìqǐ qù mǎi yìdiǎnr
   dōngxi zěnmeyàng?
B: Míngtiān jǐdiǎn? Míngtiān
   shàngwǔ wǒ yǒu yìdiǎnr shìr.
A: Nà wǒmen xiàwǔ qù.
B: Hǎo.

LESSON 7
Exercise 1
1. yíxià
2. kéyi
3. zài
4. yě

Exercise 2
1. Wǒ xuéxiàode yóuyǒngguǎn zài ...
2. Wǒ xuéxiàode yùndòng zhōngxīn ...
3. Wǒ xīngqī (number) yùndòng.
4. Wǒ zài sùshè kéyi shàngwǎng.

Exercise 3
1. A: Qǐng wèn, yùndòng zhōngxīn
      zài nǎr?
   B: Zài túshūguǎnde pángbiān. Nǐ
      zhīdào túshūguǎn zài nǎr ma?
   A: Zhīdào, xièxie.
   B: Bié kèqi.

2. A: Jīntiān xīngqījǐ?
   B: Jīntiān xīngqī'èr.
   A: Yóuyǒngguǎn jīntiān kāi ma?
   B: Wǒ yě bù zhīdào. Nǐ kéyi
      shàngwǎng kàn yíxià.
   A: Hǎo.

3. A: Nǐ jīntiān qù shàngbān ma?
   B: Jīntiān shì xīngqīliù, suóyi bú
      shàngbān.
   A: Nà, wǒmen yìqǐ qù yùndòng
      zěnmeyàng?
   B: Hǎo.

Exercise 4

1. Túshūguǎn xīngqīyī shàngwǔ qīdiǎn kāi.
2. Túshūguǎn xīngqīliù shàngwǔ bādiǎn kāi.
3. Túshūguǎn xīngqītiān xiàwǔ bù kāi.

LESSON 8
Exercise 1

1. tài
2. kěshi
3. yě
4. juéde

Exercise 2

1. Wǒ xǐhuan chī (country name) cài.
2. Wǒ píngcháng zài (place name) chīfàn.
3. Wǒ chángcháng qù wàimiànde cānguǎn chīfàn.
4. Wǒ xuéxiào shítángde cài...

Exercise 3

1. A: Nǐ xǐhuan chī Zhōngguó cài ma?
   B: Wǒ xǐhuan, wǒ yě xǐhuan chī Tàiguó cài. Nǐ chī làde cài ma?
   A: Wǒ bú tài xǐhuan.

2. A: Nǐ píngcháng zài nǎr chīfàn?
   B: Wǒ píngcháng zài shítáng chīfàn.
   A: Nǐ juéde shítángde cài zěnmeyàng?
   B: Hěn piányi, yě hěn hǎochī.

3. A: Nǐ xǐhuan chī shénme cài?
   B: Yǒude shíhou wǒ xǐhuan chī làde cài, yǒude shíhou xǐhuan chī suānde cài. Nǐ ne?
   A: Wǒ xǐhuan chī hǎochīde cài.

Exercise 4

You: Nǐ xǐhuan chī shénme cài?
Your Friend: Wǒ xǐhuan chī làde cài.
You: Nǐ píngcháng zài nǎr chīfàn?
Your Friend: Yǒude shíhou zài xuéxiàode shítáng, yǒude shíhou qù wàimiànde cānguǎn.
You: Nǐ juéde xuéxiào shítángde cài zěnmeyàng?
Your Friend: Hěn piányi, yě hěn hǎochī, kěshi yǒude shíhou tài yóule.

LESSON 9
Exercise 1

1. dàxiǎo
2. héshì
3. kéyi
4. háishì

Exercise 2

1. Wǒ píngcháng xǐhuan qù (place name) mǎi yīfu.
2. Wǒ chuān (size) hàode yīfu.
3. Wǒ xǐhuan fùxiàn/shuākǎ.

Exercise 3

1. A: Qǐng wèn, zhèijiàn kùzi yǒuméiyou xiǎohàode?
   B: Yǒu, nǐ yào-búyào shìchuān yīxià?
   A: Hǎo.

2. A: Něige bǐjiào héshì? Dàhàode háishì zhōnghàode?
   B: Dàhàode bǐjiào héshì, wǒ mǎi dàhàode.
   A: Hǎo.

3. A: Dàxiǎo zěnmeyàng?
   B: Hěn héshì. Wǒ kéyi shuākǎ ma?
   A: Dāngrán kéyi.

Exercise 4

You: Qǐngwèn, wǒ kéyi-
             bùkéyi shìchuān zhèijiàn
             kùzi?
Salesperson: Dāngrán kéyi.
You: Yǒu-méiyou dàhàode?
Salesperson: Yǒu.
You: Wǒ kéyi shuākǎ ma?
Salesperson: Kéyi.

LESSON 11
Exercise 1
1. gěi
2. wèi
3. wéi
4. xìng

Exercise 2
1. Wǒ chángcháng gěi ... dǎ diànhuà.
2. Wǒde shǒujī hàomǎ shì ...
3. Wǒ sùshède diànhuà hàomǎ shì...

Exercise 3
1. A: Wéi, qǐng wèn, Lín Xiānsheng
      zài ma?
   B: Tā xiànzài bú zài. Qǐng wèn nín
      shì něiwèi?
   A: Wǒ xìng Lǐ, shì Yīngwénxide
      jiàoshòu.

2. A: Wǒ huì qǐng Lín Xiānsheng gěi
      nín huí diàn. Nínde diànhuà
      hàomǎ shì ...?
   B: Wǒde shǒujī hàomǎ shì 138-
      8877-2266.
   A: Hǎo, wǒ zhīdàole.

3. A: Wǒ yǒu Zhōngwén míngzile.
   B: Nǐde Zhōngwén míngzi shì
      shénme?
   A: Wǒde Zhōngwén míngzi shì
      Dèng Róng.

Exercise 4
Registration Form
中文姓名 (Chinese name)：**Zhāng
                              Píng**
国别 (nationality)：**Zhōngguó**
职业别 (occupation)：**Lǎoshī**
手机号码 (cell phone number):
139-2524-1417

LESSON 12
Exercise 1
1. hé
2. xiē
3. zuì
4. zěnme

Exercise 2
1. Wǒde guójiā zuì zhòngyàode jiérì
   shì ...
2. Wǒde shēngrì shì (number) yuè
   (number) hào.
3. Xīnnián wǒmen ...

Exercise 3
1. A: Zhōngguó Nónglì Xīnnián shì
      shénme shíhou?
   B: Nónglì yīyuè yīhào.
   A: Zhōngguó rén zěnme qìngzhù?
   B: Tāmen hé jiārén yìqǐ chīfàn.

2. A: Zhōngguó rén shénme shíhou
      chī yuèbǐng?
   B: Wǒmen Zhōngqiūjié chī
      yuèbǐng. Nǐ xǐhuan yuèbǐng
      ma?
   A: Wǒ yuèláiyuè xǐhuan.

3. A: Zhōngguó zuì zhòngyàode jiérì
       shì shénme?
    B: Wǒ juéde shì Nónglì Xīnnián.
       Měiguó ne?
    A: Wǒ juéde shì Shèngdànjié.

Exercise 4

Jǐyuè Jǐhào	Shénme Jiérì
Nónglì yīyuè yīhào	Nónglì
Xīnnián	
Sìyuè wǔhào	Qīngmíngjié (Tomb-sweeping Festival)
Wǔyuè yīhào	Láodòngjié (Labor Day)
Nónglì wǔyuè wǔhào	Duānwǔjié
Nónglì bāyuè shíwǔhào	Zhōngqiūjié
Shíyuè yīhào	Guóqìngjié (National Day)

LESSON 13
Exercise 1
1. gǎnmào
2. kāi
3. duō; shǎo
4. ba

Exercise 2
1. A: Èh, zěnmele? Nǐ kànqǐlai
       yǒuyìdiǎnr bù shūfu.
    B: Wǒ gǎnmàole.
    A: Qù kànle yīshēng ma?
    B: Zuótiān hé péngyǒu qù kànle.

2. A: Yīshēng shuō shénme?
    B: Tā shuō wǒ yào duō xiūxi, duō
       hē shuǐ.
    A: Yīshēng kāile yào ma?
    B: Tā gěi wǒ kāile yìxiē yào.

3. A: Nǐ jīntiān chīle yào ma?
    B: Chīle.
    A: Nà duō xiūxi ba.
    B: Hǎo, xièxie.

Exercise 3

You:	(Friend's name), zěnmele? Nǐ kànqǐlai yǒuyìdiǎnr bù shūfu.
Your friend:	Wǒ gǎnmàole.
You:	Qù kànle yīshēng ma?
Your friend:	Shàngwǔ qù kànle.
You:	Yīshēng shuō shénme?
Your friend:	Yīshēng shuō wǒ gǎnmàole, gěi wǒ kāile yìxiē yào, yào wǒ duō xiūxi.
You:	Nà nǐ duō xiūxi ba, yě duō hē shuǐ.
Your friend:	Hǎo, xièxie.

LESSON 14
Exercise 1
1. Lái
2. yǒu
3. yào
4. cì

Exercise 2
1. A: Nǐ lái le. Qǐng jìn!
    B: Xièxie.

2. A: Yào tuō xié ma?
    B: En, zhèr yǒu tuōxié.
    A: Xièxie.

3. A: Zhè shì yìdiǎnr xiǎoyìsi.
    B: Nǐ tài kèqi le, xiàcì bié dài
       dōngxi.
    A: Náli, yīnggāide.

Exercise 3

1. You: **Zhè shì yīdiǎnr shuǐguǒ.**
   Host: **Nǐ tài kèqile.**
   You: **Nǎli, yīnggāide.**

2. You: **Zhè shì yīdiǎnr cháyè.**
   Host: **Nǐ tài kèqi le.**
   You: **Nǎli, yīnggāide.**

3. You: **Zhè shì yīdiǎnr bǐng.**
   Host: **Nǐ tài kèqi le.**
   You: **Nǎli, yīnggāide.**

4. You: **Zhè shì yīdiǎnr dàngāo.**
   Host: **Nǐ tài kèqi le.**
   You: **Nǎli, yīnggāide.**

LESSON 15
Exercise 1

1. **jiù**
2. **yǒu**
3. **bǐ**
4. **liǎng**

Exercise 2

1. **Wǒ jiā zài** (place).
2. **Wǒ jiā yǒu** (number)**ge rén.**
3. **Wǒ yǒu yīge gēge hé yīge mèimei.**
4. **Wǒ gēge** (number) **suì. Wǒ mèimei** (number) **suì.**
5. **Wǒ bàba** (number) **suì. Wǒ māma** (number) **suì.**
6. **Wǒ yǒu yíge háizi. Tā sìsuìle.**

Exercise 3

1. A: **Nǐ jiā zài nǎr?**
   B: **Wǒ jiā zài Běijīng.**
   A: **Nǐ jiā yǒu jǐge rén?**
   B: **Wǒ jiā yǒu sìge rén—bàba, māma, jiějie hé wǒ.**

2. A: **Nǐ érzi, nǚ'ér jīnnián jǐsuì le?**
   B: **Érzi bāsuì, nǚ'ér bǐ érzi xiǎo, jīnnián liùsuì.**

3. A: **Nǐ yào hē jiǔ ma?**
   B: **Bú yòng, xièxie, wǒ děi kāichē.**

Exercise 4

Wǒ jiā yǒu qīge rén.
Wǒ jiā yǒu bàba, māma, gēge, jiějie, dìdi, mèimei hé wǒ.
Wǒ jiā zài Nánjīng.
Wǒ bàba jiào Lǐ Tiān, tā wǔshísuìle.
Wǒ māma jiào Lín Lì, tā sìshíbāsuìle.
Wǒ gēge jiào Lǐ Bó, tā èrshíqīsuìle.
Wǒ jiějie jiào Lǐ Yáo, tā èrshíwǔsuìle.
Wǒ dìdi jiào Lǐ Hòu, tā èrshísuìle.
Wǒ mèimei jiào Lǐ Miào, tā shíbāsuìle.

Shéi (who)	Míngzi	Niánjì (age)
bàba	Lǐ Tiān	50
māma	Lín Lì	48
gēge	Lǐ Bó	27
jiějie	Lǐ Yáo	25
dìdi	Lǐ Hòu	20
mèimei	Lǐ Miào	18

LESSON 16
Exercise 1

1. **yào**
2. **lí**
3. **de**
4. **zuò**

Exercise 2

1. **Wǒ shì zài** (place name) **chūshēng zhǎngdàde.**
2. **Wǒ jiā zài** (place name).
3. **Zhérde qìhòu hěn hǎo, chūntiān ..., xiàtiān ..., qiūtiān ..., dōngtiān ....**
4. **Zhér chángcháng/bùcháng/bú xiàxuě.**

Exercise 3

1. A: Nǐ jiā zài Zhōngguó shénme dìfang?
   B: Wǒ jiā zài Tiānjīn.
   A: Tiānjīn lí Běijīng yuǎn-bùyuǎn?
   B: Bú tài yuǎn, zuò huǒchē chàbuduō yíge xiǎoshí.

2. A: Niǔyuēde qìhòu zěnme yàng?
   B: Dōngtiān yòu cháng yòu lěng, xiàtiān bú tài rè.
   A: Qiūtiān ne?
   B: Wǒ zuì xǐhuan qiūtiān, hěn piàoliang.

3. A: Běijīng xiàxuě ma?
   B: Duì, dōngtiān chángcháng xiàxuě. Bōshìdùn ne?
   A: Yě chángcháng xiàxuě, kěshi wǒ juéde Bōshìdùn bǐ Běijīng lěng.

Exercise 4

You: Èh, nǐ hǎo.
Passenger: Nǐ hǎo.
You: Nǐ jiào shénme míngzi?
Passenger: Wǒ jiào Xǔ Yán.
You: Nǐ shì zài nǎr chūshēng zhǎngdàde?
Passenger: Wǒ shì zài Shànghǎi chūshēng zhǎngdàde.
You: Shànghǎide qìhòu xiànzài zěnmeyàng?
Passenger: Xiànzài shì xiàtiān, hěn rè.
You: Shànghǎi lí Běijīng yuǎn-bùyuǎn?
Passenger: Shànghǎi lí Běijīng hěn jìn.
You: Zuò fēijī yào sānge xiǎoshí ma?
Passenger: Chàbuduō liǎngge xiǎoshí.

LESSON 17

Exercise 1

1. huì
2. tīngshuō
3. dào
4. děi

Exercise 2

1. Wǒ huì shuō Zhōngwén hé Yīngwén.
2. Wǒ qùguo Xiānggǎng, méi qùguo Táiwān.
3. Wǒ xǐhuan qù (place) gòuwù.
4. Cóng wǒ jiā dào Běijīng zuò fēijī yào chàbuduō sānge xiǎoshí.

Exercise 3

1. A: Qǐng wèn, nǐ huì shuō Yīngwén ma?
   B: Wǒ huì shuō yìdiǎnr Yīngwén. Nǐ huì shuō Zhōngwén ma?
   A: Wǒ bú huì.

2. A: Nǐ qùguo Niǔyuē ma?
   B: Wǒ jīnnián liùyuè qùguo, hěn yǒuyìsi.
   A: Nǐ qùguo Bōshìdùn ma?
   B: Wǒ méi qùguo Bōshìdùn.

3. A: Wǒ tīngshuō Jiùjīnshān hěn yuǎn.
   B: Cóng Běijīng dào Jiùjīnshān zuò fēijī yào duōcháng shíjiān?
   A: Chàbuduō shí'èrge xiǎoshí.

Exercise 4

Cóng...dào zuò...yào duōcháng shíjiān?
Běijīng dào Shànghǎi zuò fēijī yào <u>chàbuduō liǎngge xiǎoshí.</u>
Běijīng dào Tiānjīn kāichē yào chàbuduō <u>liǎngge xiǎoshí.</u>
Xiānggǎng dào Táiběi zuò fēijī yào <u>chàbuduō liǎngge xiǎoshí.</u>

Xiānggǎng dào Shēnzhèn kāichē <u>yào chàbuduō yīge xiǎoshí.</u>
Xiānggǎng dào Guǎngzhōu zuò huǒchē <u>yào chàbuduō liǎngge xiǎoshí.</u>
Shànghǎi dào Nánjīng zuò huǒchē <u>yào chàbuduō liǎngge xiǎoshí.</u>

LESSON 18
Exercise 1
1. Wéi
2. guìxìng
3. zài
4. qián

Exercise 2
1. Wǒ xìng (last name).
2. Cóng wǒ jiā dào jīchǎng yào sānshífēn.
3. Cóng wǒ jiā dào jīchǎng zuò chūzūqìchē yào yìbǎi yuán.

Exercise 3
1. A: Wéi, Běijīng Chūzūqìchē Gōngsī, nín hǎo.
   B: Nǐ hǎo. Wǒ míngtiān yào yíliàng chē qù jīchǎng.
   A: Méi wèntí. Nín guìxìng?
   B: Wǒ xìng Wú.

2. A: Wú Xiānsheng, míngtiān jǐdiǎn jiē nín?
   B: Xiàwǔ sāndiǎn.
   A: Zài shénme dìfang jiē nín?
   B: Běijīng Dàxué liúxuéshēng lóu.

3. A: Nínde shǒujī hàomǎ shì…
   B: Wǒde shǒujī hàomǎ shì 138-1166-5757.
   A: Hǎo, míngtiān huì zhǔnshí qù jiē nín.
   B: Xièxie.
   A: Xièxie nín.

4. A: Duìbuqǐ
   B: Méi guānxi.

Exercise 4
Receptionist: Wéi, Chūzūqìchē Gōngsī, nín hǎo.
You: Nǐ hǎo. Wǒ yào yíliàng chē qù jīchǎng.
Receptionist: Méi wèntí. Nín guìxìng?
You: Wǒ xìng Liào.
Receptionist: Liào Xiānshēng, shénme shíhou jiē nín?
You: Jīntiān xiàwǔ liǎngdiǎn.
Receptionist: Zài shénme dìfang jiē nín?
You: Fùdàn Dàxué liúxuéshēng lóu. Qǐng wèn, dào jīchǎng yào duōcháng shíjiān, duōshǎo qián?
Receptionist: Chàbuduō yào sìshífēn, yìbǎi kuài zuǒyòu. Nínde diànhuà shì…
You: Wǒde shǒujī hàomǎ shì 138-2211-0504.
Receptionist: Hǎo, jīntiān xiàwǔ huì zhǔnshí qù jiē nín.
You: Xièxie.
Receptionist: Xièxie nín, zàijiàn.
You: Zàijiàn.

LESSON 19

Exercise 1

1. qǐng
2. jìde
3. jiù
4. sòng

Exercise 2

1. Wǒ chángcháng/bù cháng/hěn shǎo qǐng péngyǒu chīfàn.
2. Wǒ chángcháng/bù cháng/hěn shǎo xiě diànzǐ yóujiàn.
3. Wǒ juéde wǒde Zhōngwén yuèláiyuè hǎole.
4. Wǒ juéde shíjiān zhēn kuài.

Exercise 3

1. A: Xièxie nǐmen jīntiān wǎnshang qǐng wǒ chīfàn.
   B: Bié kèqi. Shēngrì kuàilè!
   A: Xièxie.

2. A: Shíjiān zhēn kuài, nǐ míngtiān jiù yào huí Měiguóle.
   B: En, wǒ jìde qùnián liùyuè gāng lái, míngtiān jiù yào zǒule.
   A: Wǒmen xiě diànzǐ yóujiàn bǎochí liánluò.
   B: En, bǎochí liánluò!

3. A: Yào-búyào sòng nǐ qù jīchǎng?
   B: Bú yòng, xièxie. Wǒ yǐjīng yàole yíliàng chūzūqìchē.
   A: Nǐ míngtiān shénme shíhou zǒu?
   B: Shàngwǔ shídiǎn.

Exercise 4

(1) Gāo Zhì'ān; Lǐ Yáng
(2) Tā zài Bōshìdùn.
(3) Tāde Zhōngwényuèláiyuè hǎole.
(4) Tā xuéle hěn duō.
(5) Hǎo, bǎochí liánluò.

LESSON 20

(1) 您
(2) 你
(3) 去
(4) 请
(5) 那
(6) 吗
(7) 说
(8) 中
(9) 不
(10) 京

🎧 ONLINE AUDIO TRACK LIST

CHAPTER 1: A Basic Introduction

CHAPTER 2: The Basics

CHAPTER 3: Greetings
Ch 3: Greeting New Friends

CHAPTER 4: Introducing Yourself (I)
Ch 4: Self-Introductions

CHAPTER 5: Introducing Yourself (II)
Ch 5: Asking Questions

CHAPTER 6: Small Talk
Ch 6: Making Plans to Meet Up

CHAPTER 7: Getting Around
Ch 7: Finding Places

CHAPTER 8: Eating and Drinking
Ch 8: LunL Conversation

CHAPTER 9: Going Shopping
Ch 9: Buying Clothes

CHAPTER 10: Introduction to the Linese Writing System

CHAPTER 11: Making a Phone Call
Ch 11: Calling Manager Lin

CHAPTER 12: Holiday Celebrations
Ch 12: Important Linese Holidays

CHAPTER 13: Feeling Unwell
Ch 13: Expressing Concern

CHAPTER 14: Being Invited to the Manager's Home For Dinner (I)
Ch 14: Arriving at the Manager's Home

CHAPTER 15: Being Invited to the Manager's Home For Dinner (II)
Ch 15: Asking About Family p. 119

CHAPTER 16: Geography and Weather
Ch 16: Other Countries' Weather

CHAPTER 17: Traveling
Ch 17: Plans for Spring Break

CHAPTER 18: Arranging a Ride to the Airport
Ch 18: Calling a Taxi Company

CHAPTER 19: Farewell
Ch 19: Having a Farewell Dinner

CHAPTER 20: Introduction to The Chinese Writing System (II)

"Books to Span the East and West"

Tuttle Publishing was founded in 1832 in the small New England town of Rutland, Vermont [USA]. Our core values remain as strong today as they were then—to publish best-in-class books which bring people together one page at a time. In 1948, we established a publishing outpost in Japan—and Tuttle is now a leader in publishing English-language books about the arts, languages and cultures of Asia. The world has become a much smaller place today and Asia's economic and cultural influence has grown. Yet the need for meaningful dialogue and information about this diverse region has never been greater. Over the past seven decades, Tuttle has published thousands of books on subjects ranging from martial arts and paper crafts to language learning and literature—and our talented authors, illustrators, designers and photographers have won many prestigious awards. We welcome you to explore the wealth of information available on Asia at **www.tuttlepublishing.com**.

Published by Tuttle Publishing, an imprint of Periplus Editions (HK) Ltd.

www.tuttlepublishing.com

Copyright © 2023 Periplus Editions (HK) Ltd.
Illustration © 2023 Periplus Editions (HK) Ltd.

ISBN: 978-0-8048-5530-3

First edition

27 26 25 24 23   5 4 3 2 1
Printed in Malaysia   2305VP

Distributed by

North America, Latin America & Europe
Tuttle Publishing
364 Innovation Drive,
North Clarendon,
VT 05759-9436, USA
Tel: 1 (802) 773 8930
Fax: 1 (802) 773 6993
info@tuttlepublishing.com
www.tuttlepublishing.com

Asia Pacific
Berkeley Books Pte Ltd
3 Kallang Sector #04-01
Singapore 349278
Tel: (65) 6741 2178
Fax: (65) 6741 2179
inquiries@periplus.com.sg
www.tuttlepublishing.com

TUTTLE PUBLISHING® is a registered trademark of Tuttle Publishing, a division of Periplus Editions (HK) Ltd.

To Access the Online Audio Recordings and Flash Cards:

1. Check to be sure you have an internet connection.
2. Type the URL below into your web browser.

https://www.tuttlepublishing.com/learning-chinese

For support, you can email us at info@tuttlepublishing.com.